BLANK PAGE TO FINAL DRAFT

HOW TO PLOT, WRITE, AND EDIT A NOVEL, STEP BY STEP

BRYN DONOVAN

Blank Page to Final Draft
Copyright 2020 by Stacey Donovan

First edition, November 2020

Print: 978-1-951952-06-8
eBook: 978-0-9967152-9-4

All rights reserved. No part of this publication may be reproduced or distributed in print or electronic form without prior permission of the author.

For more writing resources and advice, visit bryndonovan.com.

For writing support, encouragement, author news, sales, and giveaways, sign up for the newsletter: https://bit.ly/2SrNjzS

TABLE OF CONTENTS

INTRODUCTION 9

SECTION I: Preparation, Planning, and Plotting 15

Step 1: Make Room 16
    Make Room in Your Mind
    Make Room in Your Schedule
    Make Sure You Have the Tools You Need
    Make Sure You Have the Information You Need
    Just Make Room
    What Else Is in Your Way?
    Finally: Skim Through This Book

Step 2: Get Genre Savvy 29
    Why Genres Matter
    Learning About Fiction Genres
    Know Your Genre
    Address Your Concerns
    Read Your Genre

Step 3: Create Your Vision 40
    If You're Truly Starting From Scratch
    Come Up With a Working Title
    Estimate Your Word Count
    Write a Short Description
    Three Common Story Issues
    Get Excited!

Step 4: Choose Your Point of View and Meet Your Characters 50
    Make Decisions About Point of View
    What Is Head-Hopping, and Why Shouldn't I Do It?
    Develop Your Main Characters

Step 5: Plot Your Novel 59
  The Index Card Method...for People Who Hate Plotting
  Other Planning Methods
  Three Things to Ask Yourself About Your Plot

Step 6: Get Feedback On Your Plot 66
  Ways of Getting Feedback
  Recharging and Renewing
  Accepting and Evaluating Feedback

Step 7: Finesse Your Plot 71

SECTION II: Writing the First Draft 73

Step 8: Write Chapter One 75
  Three Documents to Start Using Now
  Always Back Up Your Work!
  Thirty Ways to Start a Novel
  What About a Prologue?
  How Long Should My Chapters Be?

Step 9: Write Chapter Two 84
  Do You Have to Describe How Characters Look?
  How to Describe a Character's Looks in Their Point of View

Step 10: Write Chapter Three 88
  How to Format Dialogue

Step 11: First Beta Reading 92
  What If My Beta Readers Steal My Ideas?
  Questions to Ask Your Beta Readers
  Set a Deadline and Hold Them to It

Step 12: Considering Your Feedback 96
  Give Yourself a Few Days
  Recognizing and Disregarding Toxic Beta Readers
  Don't Quit Now
  Make a Revision Plan

Step 13: Reworking Chapter One 101
  Describing Settings

Step 14: Reworking Chapters Two and Three 104
    Is It Okay for Me to Write About This?

Step 15: Write to the Midpoint, Part I 108
    Writer Math
    What If My Novel Is Running Too Short?
    What If My Novel Is Running Too Long?

Step 16: Write to the Midpoint, Part II 113
    How to Stop Procrastinating
    How to Write in Deep Point of View

Step 17: Write to the Midpoint, Part III 117
    How to Stop Perfectionism From Ruining Your Progress
    Start Saving Up If Necessary

Step 18: Write to the Midpoint, Part IV 120
    Understanding Past Tense and Past Perfect Tense

Step 19: Write to the Midpoint, Part V 123
    Can I Use Song Lyrics In My Novel?
    Is It Legal to Use Brand Names In My Novel?
    Can I Write a Novel About Someone Else's Fictional Characters?

Step 20: Hit the Midpoint 126
    What Should I Do When You're Not Feeling Your Novel?

Step 21: Read Through the First Half 128

Step 22: Evaluate Your Pacing 131
    How to Evaluate the Consistency of Your Pacing
    If You Can't Tell, Ask
    Write Up Your Evaluation

Step 23: Fix Your Pacing 134
    How to Fix a Story That's Too Slow
    How To Fix a Story That's Too Rushed
    How to Fix Inconsistent Pacing

Step 24: Fix Those One or Two Things 136
    More Writer Math

Step 25: Write to the End, Part I 138
   How to Use All Five Senses in Your Writing

Step 26: Write to the End, Part II 141
   What's Wrong With Adverbs?

Step 27: Write to the End, Part III 144
   How to Use Writing Sprints
   Internet Blockers

Step 28: Write to the End, Part IV 146
   Are the Demons Trying to Lurk Back In?

Step 29: Write to the End, Part V 149
   How to Recognize and Avoid Comma Splices

Step 30: Write to the End, Part VI 151
   Self-Care for Writers

Step 31: Write to the End, Part VII 154
   4 Tips for Writing Fight Scenes

Step 32: Write to the End, Part VIII 156
   Avoiding Passive Voice

Step 33: Write to the End, Part IX 159
   Affirmations for Writers

Step 34: Write to the End, Part X 162
   Should I Use a Pen Name?
   Considerations When Choosing a Pen Name
   Don't Catfish
   Pen Names and Submitting

Step 35: Finish It! 166

SECTION III: Revising and Editing 167

Get It in Shape! 169

Step 36: Clarify the First Character Arc 170

Step 37: Clarify the Second Character Arc 172

Step 38: Fine-Tune Main Characters' Speech and Behavior 173
    Overfamiliar Dialogue
    Do Women and Men Always Speak and Act Differently?
    A Few More Considerations
    Why This Step Matters

Step 39: Pump It Up, Part I 179
    The Billboard Fill-In-The-Blank Exercise
    Bringing Your Draft to Life
    Stuck? Make a Quick List

Step 40: Pump It Up, Part II 183
    Do It Again
    Get Your Beta Readers Lined Up

Step 41: It's Beta Reader Time! 184
    Do You Need a Sensitivity Reader?
    While You're Waiting, Check Your Point of View

Step 42: While You're Waiting, Check Your Chapter Lengths, Chapter Breaks, and Timeline 187
    Checking the Chapter Lengths
    Teasing the Chapter Endings
    Fixing Your Timeline
    Making the Passage of Time Clear

Step 43: Read Over Your Feedback 191
    What If I Can't Get My Beta Readers to Read It?

Step 44: Revise Based on Beta Reader Feedback, Part I 193

Steps 45 and 46: Revise Based on Beta Reader Feedback, Parts II and III 194

Step 47: Copyediting, Part I: Trim Where Needed 195

Step 48: Copyediting, Part II: Cleaning Up 197
    Clean Up Your Dialogue Tags
    Eliminate Most Instances of Passive Voice
    Replace Many Weak Verbs

Step 49: Copyediting, Part III: Quit Repeating Yourself ... 201

Step 50: Copyediting, Part IV: Read Aloud and Fix As You Go ... 202

Step 51: Send It to Proofreading ... 203

Step 52: Get to Your FINAL DRAFT! ... 205
    Back Up Your Novel and Print It Out
    What If I'm Self-Publishing?
    Do I Need to Copyright My Novel?
    CELEBRATE!

About the Author ... 207

INTRODUCTION

WELCOME! TODAY'S AN EXCITING DAY. You're starting to write a great new book. It might be your first one, or it might be your best one yet.

One year from today…or perhaps much sooner…you could be holding a new novel manuscript in your hands.

Take a minute to imagine it. It'll be a hefty stack of paper…maybe 250, 300, 400 pages. It'll be finished, edited, and even proofread: ready to send to agents or publishers, or to publish yourself. You'll feel proud of your accomplishment.

Many of us dream of completing a novel, though few actually do it. Those of us who haven't been able to complete one often blame ourselves for not having more inspiration or discipline. Or sometimes, we blame our circumstances, saying it's impossible to finish a novel while going to school or holding down a full-time job.

But none of these things may be entirely to blame. Writing a book is a big, complicated project, and many of us don't have the framework or the structure we need.

Some of us have ideas, but we aren't sure how to actually begin.

Some of us have been told, "Just write!" So we do. We get fifty or one hundred pages in, and then can't figure out what to do next.

And some of us write complete exuberant, messy rough drafts of novels…and then don't know how to edit them.

Because writing a novel is such a big project, many of us also aren't sure how to fit it into our busy lives.

Even people who have already written several novels sometimes look for a more structured way to approach the work and balance it against their day jobs, their parenting, and all the other demands on their time.

HOW THIS BOOK CAME ABOUT

Blank Page to Final Draft includes a schedule I made for myself after years of never finishing a draft...and then finishing one that was such a hot mess, I didn't know what to do with it.

The first time I followed this schedule, I wrote and edited a book in exactly one year and got my first publishing contract. It was from a small publisher, but for me, it was a big deal—a dream come true. I followed the same process for two other novels: one I also wrote in a year's time, and one I wrote in under six months.

I've also written a couple of novels that I worked on intermittently over the course of a few years. So I'm *not* saying this is the only way to write a novel, and anyone who says there's one perfect way to do it doesn't know what they're talking about.

As an executive editor in publishing, I've talked to a lot of people who are looking for a blueprint about how to plan a novel, structure their time, and reach their writing goals. I've also noticed that many new authors make the same kinds of mistakes...and I understand, because I've made every single one of them in the past, myself.

This book does three things:

- It breaks down a daunting project into smaller, manageable steps.
- It addresses all kinds of common issues, questions, and pitfalls to help you improve both your story and your writing style.
- It gives you support and inspiration all throughout the process.

If you already have a completed manuscript, you can use section three as an editing guide. For many people, revising is the most confusing part! I break it down step by step so it's not overwhelming.

If you've written novels in the past, but you've hit a low period in your author journey—or you're coming back to writing after not doing it for a long while—you may worry that you've lost your spark. You haven't. Creativity is never gone for good. This book can help that spark glow brighter again.

If you've never completed a polished novel before, you may have gotten discouraged. You may have even thought that if you could do it, you would've done it by now.

Forget all those negative thoughts. That's the past. You can do this. You can start today.

HOW TO USE THIS BOOK

The Regular Pace

If you're truly starting with a blank page and you want a finished, polished manuscript in your hands one year from now, do one step a week for the next year. You'll likely be able to balance this with a day job, a full-time school schedule, or family responsibilities (but if you're juggling more than one of the above, you may need to take longer.)

The Fast Pace

Do two steps a week instead of one step and have a completed, polished novel in six months' time.

Your Pace

You may be a speed demon who can do several steps a week. There are no limits. Go as fast as you can!

Alternately, you may find that one year is *way* too fast for you—because of your hectic life, your own creative process, a personal crisis, or other reasons. You might fall behind the one-step-a-week pace.

If this is your experience, you'll be in great company.

As a writer, it's easy to feel like you're too slow and that everybody else can write faster than you. The truth is, many people write slowly. You may have good reasons for it.

You may have a more complicated story…and if you're an epic fantasy, science fiction, or historical fiction author, you know all about this. And of course, may have a more complicated *life*. If you have a demanding day job, children at home, caregiving duties, or an illness, you face very real challenges, both in terms of time and energy. Big changes in your life, health concerns, and personal crises can all slow down your writing.

All that aside, you may have a more contemplative creative process, and there's nothing wrong with that. Sometimes this can lead to deeper insights and more memorable storytelling.

Give yourself a break and avoid comparing yourself to other writers. If you must compare, though, think about your favorite authors of all time. I bet at least some of them are *not* super-fast!

Unless a publisher has given you a deadline, your pace is your business, and no one else has the right to judge. Progress is progress, and as long as you're sticking with it and moving forward, you should feel great about yourself. You're on your own path, and your own rewards are waiting for you.

The Checklist

At the end of each step in this book, I've included a checklist of tasks. Doing all the tasks for each step will keep you on track.

THE BEST TIME TO START MAY BE NOW

There's always a tendency to put off our biggest dreams.

"I'll start this on January 1," you might say. "It'll be my project for that year." Okay, if it's the end of November and you're involved in six different holiday celebrations, that's probably sensible. But if it's April or August, do you really want to wait that long? You might decide, "I'll do this once things settle down at work." Are you sure they ever will?

You don't need to wait until you're absolutely sure of what you're doing. If everyone did that, we wouldn't have many books. You don't need to wait until you've got things planned out, because the whole first section is about planning.

If you're doing one step a week, you might want to start this coming Monday. I recommend diving in unless you have a good reason not to—for instance, if you're doing this with a friend or a group, which I'll talk about next.

CONSIDER STARTING A GROUP

If you know other writers who share your goals, you might want to consider doing the *Blank Page to Final Draft* program along with them! You can resolve as a group to do a step a week (or however fast or slow you want to take it). Every week, you can check in and discuss how it went.

There are a lot of advantages to doing BPFD as a group:

- It'll keep you accountable, because you don't want to be That Person in the group who's always falling behind.
- It'll keep you positive, because you'll get encouragement from others for hitting your marks.
- When you do hit a snag, someone else who's doing the same thing as you might have good advice for you.
- You'll have built-in beta readers…and beta readers are crucial to this process.
- You'll grow closer to the people you write with, and friendships are important to happiness.

Groups being what they are, you'll probably have some people who intend to do it, but don't follow through. That's okay. If you can find just one, two, or three people who are as committed as you are, there will be almost nothing that can stop you.

SECTIONS I, II, AND III

Section I outlines personal preparation, plotting, planning, and character development.

Section II is all about actually writing the first draft.

Section III is dedicated to revising, editing, and proofreading. Writers often underestimate how much time it takes to shape a rough draft into a finished story. This section will help you turn your diamond in the rough into a story that sparkles.

It's your novel.

You may find yourself wanting to skip or change some of the steps in this book. If you've never completed a novel before, I recommend at least giving each step a try. You might think, "That's not for me," but the truth is, you haven't figured out what works for you yet. We all have a tendency to avoid the more difficult and analytical parts of writing—sometimes labeling them "boring"—but those can turn out to be crucial steps. They're often not so difficult or boring, after all, once we're in the middle of doing them.

In the end, of course, you can work however you want. This is a book full of advice; you may decide that some of the advice is not for you. You may be adapting the schedule in the book to a partially finished manuscript. Your project may have unique needs, and you're the best person to figure those out.

Let's go ahead and get started. And congratulations in advance on your fantastic, polished novel.

SECTION I: PREPARATION, PLANNING, AND PLOTTING

In this section, you're going to form a clear vision for your novel and set yourself up for success.

You may feel impatient in this section. I understand and admire the urge to dive right in! However, I believe the planning at the beginning may prevent you from getting stuck halfway through.

You may even feel *hostile* toward this section. I'll be prompting you to think about things like genre and word count before you even start writing!

Why am I doing that? After all, lots of people out there will tell you: don't worry at the beginning about word count! Don't worry about genre! You can figure that out later!

But many writers finish a whole manuscript and then realize they can't make the leap between writing and publication...or writing and successful self-publishing. All along, they weren't thinking too much about the end result, and now that it's time to sell the book to an agent, an editor, or a wide audience, it's almost impossible to do so. In my day job in publishing, I see this *all the time,* and it breaks my heart.

Having a clear idea of where your book fits in the market doesn't guarantee a publishing contract or a lot of sales. It does make those things more likely.

With writing and everything else in life, it boils down to this: if you like the results you're getting, keep doing what you're doing. If you're not satisfied with the results, try something new.

The personal preparation in this section may seem the most unnecessary. However, it may lead you to confront issues that have hampered your creative process for *years* and overcome them once and for all.

STEP 1: MAKE ROOM

In this first step, you're going to prepare your mind, your relationships with others, your schedule, and more so you can write your novel.

You may identify factors that have held you back in your writing in the past. Facing up to some of these things may not be easy. If you acknowledge they exist, you'll realize you have to change them…and change can be uncomfortable. But change may be necessary to take your writing to a whole new level.

MAKE ROOM IN YOUR MIND

Before anything else, you need to make sure that you have the right mental attitude. Many of us face very tangible challenges in our writing, but the toughest challenges can be our own thoughts.

If you're going to write a great novel, you don't have room for defeatist beliefs. They're too hard for your brain to deal with while it's trying to come up with a story.

How do you evict negative thoughts, though? You do it by noticing when they crop up and substituting other thoughts in their place.

Here are some common negative thoughts people have about their writing. See if any of them resonate with you!

1. It's hard to keep writing because I know I'm not very good.
This trips people up a lot, particularly people who are newer to novel writing. When you're learning how to do something, you're usually not fantastic at it right away. You don't show up at your first foreign language class and start speaking fluently or go to a ski slope for the first time in your life and zoom down the hardest slope.

As toddlers and children, we're always doing things we're bad at. Walking, getting dressed, reading and writing—we're bad at everything! As adults, we're not as used to being bad at something, but with writing, we have to accept that we're not going to start out great.

To get better at writing, you can read a lot of craft books, attend seminars and workshops, and make notes of passages in books you love. All of these can help a lot! But when it comes down to it, you need to be willing to write even when you know it's not going to be perfect.

There's no way around this. Believe me, if there were, one of us would've figured it out by now. The very experience of writing and then editing later is how we get better.

Some of us take it personally if we can't write great stories right away, though. We get the wrong idea that it means something shameful about us as a person.

Why is that? Maybe if we love books, we feel like we ought to instinctively understand how they're written. In my own case, this wasn't true at all. I've always been a voracious reader, but when it came to writing, I still didn't understand some very basic things without reading books about writing and taking some seminars at writing conferences.

We might also have the idea that mediocre writing somehow means we're a mediocre *person*...that we're lacking in originality, style, creativity, intelligence, or talent.

This is pure nonsense.

Writing is a skill. Some people have more natural ability for it than others, but most people grossly overestimate the importance of raw talent and grossly underestimate the importance of study and practice.

The quality of your writing has nothing to do with your worth as a person. Don't get these two things confused. You could write the most godawful novels in the world, one after another, and be an intelligent, warm, loving, inspiring, amazing person. Conversely, you could write masterpieces and be a horrible human (a few authors have actually proved this).

This can be a painful and difficult topic, because many creative people were drawn to creating precisely because they had poor self-worth. Their talent was the one thing that earned them praise at home or at school. It was their way of proving that, despite what others perceived as shortcomings — their supposed unattractiveness, their awkwardness, their mental health issue, and so on — they had value.

You're already cool. You're already unique. You're already worthy of love.

If you're writing a bad draft, be proud of yourself. You're on your way to a good draft.

Try thinking this instead:

It's easy to keep writing because I'm getting better all the time.

or simply:

I'm getting good at this.

---

2. Writing is probably a wasted effort. I'll never be truly successful.
In a culture obsessed with wealth and fame, it's easy for us to unconsciously decide that these are the only two good reasons to do anything.

Of course, we know better. Some of the most worthwhile things we can do in life—play with a child, take a walk in nature—won't make us a bit more rich or famous.

A few times, I've made quilts for other people, my husband, and myself. The fabric was quite expensive, and I spent many, many hours on each quilt. I am not a good quilter (though I'd get better if I made more of them). No one would ever pay me real money for one of my quilts or give it even an honorable mention in the least competitive quilt show around. I still found it satisfying to complete them, and my family members and friends enjoyed them, too. It wasn't a waste of time. I feel the same way about each novel, whether it found a large audience or not.

As I'm writing this, I just got back from the beach where a group of dozens of people were running together, training for a marathon. The runners were of all ages and all body types. Frankly, I doubt any of them would *win* a marathon. None of them will make money doing it. It's satisfying to accomplish something difficult like finishing a marathon, and finishing a novel is a similar challenge in many ways.

But if you don't believe finishing a novel is in itself a worthy goal, and you're determined to attain commercial success, critical acclaim, or both, then you'll especially want to be thorough with the early steps in this book. Beginning with the end in mind—thinking about your book's concept and its market—will help you do that, and it'll help you feel more confident about what you're doing.

And try thinking one of these things instead:

The work I do today will help me achieve my dreams tomorrow.

Time spent on being creative is always time well-spent.

---

3. I should be doing things for my family instead of writing.

Parents often feel guilty about pursuits that take time away from their spouses and their children. They worry that they're being selfish, a bad parent, or a bad partner.

It wasn't always this way. At the age of five or six, I was fixing my own breakfast. All the children I knew had hours and hours of time to themselves, and as a kid who loved reading, writing, coloring, and playing with dolls, I liked it that way. As we got older, on weekends and in the summer, we had the run of the neighborhood during the day and came home for dinner. I'm not a parent myself, so I'm no expert, but my personal opinion is that children can benefit from a certain amount of self-sufficiency.

Parents suffer under a much heavier burden of expectation these days. It seems to me as though some mothers, in particular, feel guilty if they're doing *anything* that isn't in the service of their children.

Historically, most writers have been parents. Think of your ten or twenty favorite books of all time: most of them probably wouldn't exist if the author had decided it was selfish to work on their book instead of doing more for their kids.

Being a parent means you may have a lot of demands on your time, and we'll talk about that more in just a minute. But it doesn't mean you should feel guilty about writing.

You probably want your children to pursue what they love and follow their dreams. There's no better way to teach that than by example.

Try thinking things like this instead:

I'm a parent, and I'm also a writer.

I set a wonderful example for my children by making time for what makes me happy.

4. Writing is too hard for me because I have an attention disorder.

I have a severe attention deficit disorder, so I understand the struggle. I can still finish projects, and you can, too.

Listening to music while you write, doing short stints (fifteen or twenty minutes; set an alarm), and taking a short walk between writing stints are all things that could help you concentrate. You might also talk to a doctor about medication for ADHD. But whatever you do, don't make up your mind that it's an insurmountable issue.

Try thinking things like this instead:
I find ways to concentrate on my writing.
My daydreams sometimes fuel my creative work.

---

5. Writing is too hard for me because I have depression or anxiety.

A lot of people struggle with depression and anxiety, and it seems like creative people are more susceptible to it than most. If you are struggling with severe, life-threatening depression, then you probably *aren't* going to be able to write a novel and you should only be focused on getting better. Nothing matters more than your well-being. Reach out and get the help you need. You deserve it.

If you have mild depression or anxiety, then you can probably still write a novel. Many successful novelists deal with the same things. You may actually find that the project helps you feel better. It's going to be important to approach it as something you do for enjoyment rather than an extra burden or expectation you're putting on yourself.

Try thinking this instead:
I have challenges, but I'm still writing my story.

With writing, it's easy for us to fall into all-or-nothing thinking. This can also be true when it comes to school, work, and additional personal pursuits. Our inner drama queen or king kicks in. "What do I love more—my family or my writing?!" "I can't write—if I don't concentrate on my job, I'll get fired and I'll never get another job again and I'll be homeless!"

Some of us may fall into this thinking because we long to write, but we're scared. We find easy, respectable excuses for not doing something we're secretly dying to do.

We may also think in black-and-white terms because we have trouble figuring out how to structure our writing time. Because it's complicated, we may feel that it requires our full attention. But this book structures your novel writing for you.

I probably didn't cover all the self-defeating thoughts and beliefs you have about your writing. Write them down, and then write down the belief you're going to replace them with, like I've done above.

Make space in your mind for your intention—whether it's to complete your first novel, or to write your best one yet.

Negative thoughts are like house guests who are secretly robbing you of all your best stuff. They will steal your future novel from right under you if you aren't careful. You've entertained these thoughts for so long. You're probably even getting bored of them. It's time to show them the door.

MAKE ROOM IN YOUR SOCIAL CIRCLE

Keep Quiet Around the Naysayers
Maybe you've cleared some of the negative messages from your own head...but what if you're getting them from the people around you?

Hopefully, your friends and family will support you in pursuing your goals. That's what friends and family are supposed to do, after all. But it doesn't always work out that way. You may have people in your life who say discouraging things.

"Don't quit your day job!" they may say, with a chortle. Why does that sting so much if it's just a joke and if you weren't planning on quitting your day job, anyway? Because it's not just a joke. It's their way of saying, *Don't think you're going to be good at this.* It's mean and dismissive.

Other people—including other writers!—may make fun of your story. In so many words, they may say fantasy novels are overdone or nobody will ever want to read a novel about a middle-aged man or an elderly woman.

Why do some people want to predict you'll fail as a writer?

They're scared you're going to succeed.

If you finish a novel, what does that mean for them? It means maybe they could pursue a dream, too, even if it's difficult. And they may not want to face that. It's a ton of work to pursue a lifelong goal. It's much easier and more comfortable to avoid it (even if, deep down, it hurts your soul not to go after it).

Other writers can be particularly critical. If they've had challenges and disappointments, then by God, they want you to know you're going to have them, too.

Don't discuss your work with anyone who disparages your writing aspirations. If you live with someone who does that, it may not be possible to keep your writing a secret, but you don't have to talk about it all the time.

You may feel the urge to change someone's mind and convince them your project is worthwhile. Forget about it. You've probably heard of the verse in the Bible about not casting your pearls before swine. The verse ends by saying, "…they may trample them under their feet, and turn and tear you to pieces." Regardless of your personal beliefs, it's a powerful warning…and a wise one.

Find Your Pack

Six weeks from now (or sooner, if you're going fast), you're going to need at least a couple of beta readers, and preferably more. "Beta readers" are people who read an early draft of your work—the "beta version"—and give you feedback. Ideally, they should be people who read a lot and are good at articulating what's working in a story and what isn't.

I strongly recommend lining up several beta readers if you can. For one thing, at least one or two of them will not follow through on their promise to read your work and give you feedback. That's human nature. It's just like when you throw a party and several people RSVP but then don't show up. (Everyone's had that experience, right? It's not just me?)

The other reason to get several beta readers is that you'll get a better sense of what's working and what isn't. If you have one beta reader and they hate a line of dialogue, you might be inclined to cut it. If you have five beta readers and four of them point out how much they *loved* that line, you'll know that it's probably okay to leave it in.

If you can find other writers who also need feedback, you can become *critique partners* and give each other help. While most beta readers are giving feedback out of the goodness of their hearts, with critique partners, it's ideally an equal exchange benefitting both people.

Even before you need beta readers, it helps a lot to have connections with fellow writers. You may already have a pack of writer friends, and if you do, you know how precious they are. If you don't, finding one may seem like a difficult task. Other like-minded writers are out there, though, and it may take a few tries, but you can find them and connect with them.

Here are some ways to look for your pack.

*Do an online search for your city (or a nearby city) + "writing group." See what turns up.

*Do searches on Facebook for Facebook writing groups. Search "novel writing group" or your genre + "writing group."

*Ask your local library for suggestions.

Although some fellow writers can be unsupportive, fellow writers may also become the best friends you've ever had. (I even married one!)

Reaching out can be difficult for shy writers, but it's worth it. This journey is going to be a whole lot easier if you don't take it alone. Finding your pack is another way of making room in your life for writing.

MAKE ROOM IN YOUR SCHEDULE

One of the biggest barriers I hear about writing is, "I don't have time." For many of us, time is a scarce commodity, and this is a very real challenge.

At the same time, let's be honest. Many of us who say "I don't have time" found the time to spend hours watching TV, browsing online, or playing video games.

Some people will say, "But I need that time to de-stress!" In fact, the internet in particular is likely *adding* to your stress. Many sites are designed to obtain purchases, comments, and clicks, and the most common way to get them is to play on your anxiety or stir your rage. Every time you get mad at a headline and click on a link to read more of that inflammatory column or article, you help a corporation rake in advertising dollars. And what do you get out of it? Depression, heightened resentments toward others, the loss of your peace of mind… and a loss of creativity. Is that a fair trade?

In fiction, characters' decisions make them who they are. The same is true in real life. You may need to ask yourself, every day, questions like: "Do I want to be a TV watcher? Do I want to be someone who spends their free time posting bitter comments online? Or do I want to be a prolific writer?"

If you really want to know where your time goes, find a time-tracking app and track every minute of your day for several days. You may be surprised at how much time gets wasted on things that aren't a priority for you.

Unless you don't have a job or children, you'll have to rein in the time you spend on things like TV and the internet. The most straightforward way to do it is to limit yourself to thirty minutes or an hour every day. At first, you may not like this rationing. But if you want to take your writing to the next level, you're going to have to make changes, and in a month or two, wasting less time will feel normal.

If you have children, you may or may not be able to adjust how much time that takes. If you can hire a babysitter for every Saturday afternoon so you can write, do it. If you've volunteered for something that turned out to be an unrewarding time suck, quit—or let people know now that you'll be quitting at the end of the month, the season, or the semester.

Whether you're a parent or not, you may have other claims on your time that need reevaluating. You can't do it all, and you're making writing a priority. Pare down elsewhere to make room for it.

When are you going to write? In the morning, before anyone else in your house is awake? This can be a great time, because you're less likely to get interrupted. On your lunch hour at work? After dinner? All day Sunday, every Sunday? Make a plan.

MAKE SURE YOU HAVE THE TOOLS YOU NEED

For a first draft you can edit, you need to use a personal computer with a standard word processing program. It's okay if you like to write longhand first, like I do, but you'll need to then type the pages you write into a master document as you go.

Even the most basic laptop computer will be adequate for writing your novel. If you don't have one and can't afford one, your local library may be an option. You might also be able to use a friend's or family member's computer.

Beyond the basics, now is a great time to treat yourself to tools that'll motivate you. You might consider any of the following:

- a fat new spiral notebook
- a pack of your favorite pens
- a coffee mug with your favorite writing quote on it
- a bulletin board for notes and pictures that inspire you
- essential oils in a diffuser to help with your mental focus (try rosemary, lemon, clary sage, cypress, or some blend of them)
- headphones or earbuds, to listen to instrumental music or "white noise" and help you concentrate (hint: there are lots of recordings, many several hours long, of nature sounds and other white noise available free online)
- your favorite writing snack or treat!

Getting yourself an extra writing-related gift or two is a great way to send a message to yourself that your writing matters.

One tool you may also want to get is the most recent edition of the *Chicago Manual of Style*. This is the guide that most fiction editors default to in matters of proper grammar, punctuation, and usage, although most publishing houses have personal style preferences as well.

MAKE SURE YOU HAVE THE INFORMATION YOU NEED

Let's say you're writing a work of historical fiction, science fiction, a story about a profession you don't know much about, or a story set in a place you don't know well. If you haven't done your research yet, you're going to need to spend a few weeks in step 1. Nonfiction books, well-researched novels, movies, and even online videos may help you amass the knowledge you need.

If you're writing a fantasy novel, you probably need to do some world-building. You should have some idea of the governments, laws, and customs in your make-believe world. What do people eat? What do they wear? What are their homes like? You need to understand the basic cultures of the different groups of beings and how they interact. You may have to figure out the possibilities and limitations of magic in your world. You might even want to draw a map.

You don't have to know *everything* to get started, though. Until you start writing, you won't even know exactly what you need to know. Right now, you just need enough information to feel grounded.

I've heard of writers getting lost for months in their research… or spending *years* on their world-building. At a certain point, research and world-building become a respectable front for procrastination, so don't get stuck here for too long.

JUST MAKE ROOM

Where are you going to write your novel? You need a clean, quiet place to work.

I actually recommend giving your whole home a good cleaning. Clutter can block creativity. Preparing a space for your writing sends a profound message to yourself that your project is worth something. It's like cleaning up before an honored houseguest arrives.

However, if it would take months to get your whole place clean, it's okay! You just need one space that is cleaned up to be your place to write. This could mean making your bed and cleaning off the table next to it, or vacuuming the couch and clearing off the coffee table.

WHAT ELSE IS IN YOUR WAY?

Take a couple of minutes to think about whether there are any other roadblocks in your life keeping you from doing the best writing you can do…or keeping you from doing any writing at all, as the case may be.

If you drink three beers after work every day and it makes you too groggy to feel like writing, that's a problem. You'll need to change it.

If you have a history of never finishing a story because you're always abandoning it for a shiny new idea you decide is better, you're going to have to make up your mind that you're going to finish…no matter if you think of one *hundred* better ideas in the meantime.

If you're a writer, and you're also trying to learn a foreign language and run a blog *and* sell homemade dolls at craft shows…you're going to have to put a couple of things on the back burner, trusting that there will be time to do them later.

FINALLY: SKIM THROUGH THIS BOOK

Most chapters in this book contain mini-lessons about writing. Depending on your project and your needs as a writer, some of them may be things you want to consider sooner rather than later. If you take a couple of hours to skim through the pages, topics that are particularly useful to you will probably jump out at you. They'll help you as you plan your novel and begin the first draft.

Step 1 may not feel like progress at all. In fact, it's a breakthrough.

If you've done all these things, you've unlocked more of your potential as a writer. You're already—as of today—on a whole new level.

Great job! You've set yourself up to do the best writing of your life so far, and you're going to be very excited to see what you can accomplish.

CHECKLIST FOR STEP 1

- [ ] I've examined all the negative thoughts I have about writing, and I've come up with new, positive beliefs to replace them.
- [ ] I've recognized the naysayers in my life, and I've resolved to not discuss my writing with them.
- [ ] I have a pack of fellow writers *or* I've taken a first step to finding one.
- [ ] I've given serious thought about the choices I make every day, and I'm making at least two changes in my life to allow me to write more.
- [ ] I know when I'm going to work on my writing.
- [ ] I have the tools I need to write—or at least, I have access to them.
- [ ] I have at least one designated place, either in my home or outside of it, for writing.
- [ ] I've skimmed through this book.

STEP 2: GET GENRE SAVVY

IN THIS STEP, YOU'RE GOING to do a *lot* of reading. You've probably heard before that reading is essential to good writing, and it's absolutely true. Of course, if you're interested in writing, chances are good you like to read, anyway. You'll probably enjoy this!

WHY GENRES MATTER

In fiction, a *genre* is a category defined by the plot and the style of the book. It defines how a publisher markets a novel.

When I first started figuring out how to write a novel, I didn't consider genres at all. This was a big mistake. You always have a better chance of success if you begin with a clear vision in mind of what you want to accomplish.

Every genre carries its own expectations. A thriller needs to be exciting, as the name implies. You can't write a mystery and not solve the murder at the end—your readers will throw the book across the room. If it's a romance, the couple needs to live happily ever after—no exceptions! (Yes, you can write a tragic love story, but that would be a different genre altogether.)

Knowing your genre up front will help you write your story. It'll keep you from going off the rails. Besides, when people ask you what kind of book you're writing, it's nice to have an answer.

You'll need to know the genre eventually, because the editors and agents you submit to expect that in a query. If you are self-publishing, retail channels will force you to put it in some kind of category.

But maybe you're thinking…

What if my novel doesn't fit into a genre? What if it's something the world has never seen before?

Respectfully, this is unlikely. Genres are broad, there are lots of them, and they have developed over decades and centuries. There's a place for your book in there. It's possible that you have a blend of genres, such as *literary thriller* or *paranormal Western*, that will be cross-listed in two or more categories. Even then, if you look, you can probably find other books that straddle genres in the same way.

You might be thinking: how would I know what genre I'm writing? I don't even have a story idea yet!

That's totally fine! Familiarize yourself with genres anyway. You may find one genre is calling your name, and the exercises to come are likely to inspire you.

Here's one quick exercise that might help you figure out what genre would suit you, though. Really quickly, make a list of ten movies you love.

Don't think about it too hard! You're not making a list of your definitive top ten favorites. Just write down ten movies that you love, as fast as you can.

Got them? Okay, great! Do the same thing with TV shows.

Now, look over your lists. Does one genre or category keep cropping up again and again?

If the movies you wrote down are critically acclaimed art-house films, you probably want to consider literary fiction. If you wrote down several thrillers, on the other hand, that should tell you something. If you love a bunch of shows about paranormal matters, you may want to consider urban fantasy or paranormal romance.

You may even notice themes that come up again and again. Whether you gravitate toward coming-of-age narratives, stories about brothers, or exotic locales, you may identify elements you'd love to include in your own story.

LEARNING ABOUT FICTION GENRES

Here's the first way I recommend to get to know fiction genres: look at BISAC subject headings for fiction. These are developed by the Book Industry Study Group for shelving and marketing books, and you can find the fiction list online. These change from time to time, so search "BISAC subject headings" plus the current year.

When you pull up the complete list, you may see that the project you have in mind could fit in three, four, or even more categories. That's fine! Your book may be a combination of a few of them.

Some of these subject codes are, strictly speaking, categories rather than genres, but they can still give you an idea of where your book fits in the market.

The other way to familiarize yourself with fiction genres is to peruse fiction categories on Amazon. It probably won't take you long to figure out where the project you have in mind fits.

You'll notice on Amazon that genres may have many subgenres…and sub-subgenres. For example, "culinary mystery" is usually a type of cozy mystery, which is a subgenre of mystery.

When you're starting a book, it's helpful to have a rough word count in mind, and some genres tend to run longer than others. I'll go over some of the most common genres later in this chapter.

I'll also include the typical length. However, desired length does vary from publisher to publisher, and the typical novel length in a genre can change over time.

Your project may combine a few genres. Even in this case, one genre will probably be primary. If you're writing historical fantasy, fantasy readers are probably the core audience, although many fans of historical fiction will likely be intrigued as well. If you're writing a young adult time travel story, it's likely a young adult novel first and foremost. Think about how your story would get pitched to a publisher and who it would get marketed to, and make your best guess.

Here's an overview of some of the most common genres in fiction. It's not a complete list. You'll need to do your own research!

Literary

Literary fiction intends to be art. It may have a focus on the thoughts of the characters, and it may explore bigger issues of society, politics, and morals. The writing style may be more original, artistic, or challenging than in other categories. The ending is somewhat more likely to be sad, bittersweet, inconclusive, or ambiguous than it is in commercial fiction. 70,000 – 100,000 words is a good range, but in this category in particular, the word count varies quite a bit.

Upmarket

This is basically literary fiction with broad appeal. It's somewhat more likely than literary fiction to have a conclusive ending. If you think of the types of books that people often choose to read and discuss in book clubs, that might give you a good idea of what "upmarket fiction" is. "Upmarket women's fiction" is a common categorization. 70,000 – 100,000 words is a good range as well.

Fantasy

The subgenres of fantasy include epic fantasy and urban fantasy. 90,000 - 120,000 words is a typical range. They run longer than some genres because it takes some time on the page to build the imaginary world. Keep in mind that in every genre, famous authors are more likely than debut authors to publish very long books.

Science Fiction

Space opera and time travel are two examples of subgenres. Like fantasy, science fiction can run long: 90,000 – 120,000 words is a reasonable target for a debut novel.

Young Adult

Often known as YA. Young adult fiction began as fiction for readers in their teens, featuring teenage protagonists. Young adult novels may encompass another genre, such as YA romance or YA historical. 50,000 to 80,000 words is a good length.

Historical

Historical fiction novels may run between 80,000 and 110,000 words. Note that other genres on this list may be contemporary or historical.

Horror

Horror novels are written with the specific intention of scaring the reader. They may explore life philosophies or tacitly critique societal norms. Ghosts, monsters, demons, and killers often feature in horror fiction. 70,000 – 90,000 words is a good working range.

Mystery
A mystery story has to lay out the puzzle to be solved—such as a murder, a stolen diamond—and give enough clues to engage the reader to try to solve it. At the end, the mystery is solved, and the readers find out if they guessed right. Hardboiled mystery, cozy mystery, noir, and historical mystery are a few smaller categories within this genre. 60,000 – 80,000 words is a typical range.

Thriller
Thrillers have exciting plots and strong external conflict. The stories may involve espionage, crime, conspiracy, or large-scale disaster. 80,000—90,000 words is a good range here, too.

Suspense
What's the difference between a suspense novel and a thriller? Thrillers are more action-oriented, while suspense novels keep you on the edge of your seat, knowing danger is around the corner. 80,000—90,000 is a good range for the word count.

Romance
A romance novel features a central love story with a happy ending, no exceptions. Romance can range from G-rated to X-rated. The subgenres include contemporary romance, romantic suspense, historical romance, inspirational (meaning "Christian") romance, paranormal romance, fantasy romance, and science fiction romance. The word count can range from 55,000 (typical for some Harlequin series romance, for example) to 90,000 words.

Western
Westerns are sent in the American West and usually take place in the 19th century or early 20th century. Traditionally, these novels have been short, so 45,000 – 75,000 words is a good target. (Of course, if you're writing Western Literary Fiction, like Cormac McCarthy's *All The Pretty Horses*, your book may be longer.)

Christian Fiction
This is a broad category characterized by strong elements of Christianity. Redemption is likely part of a character arc. This category includes many different types of stories, so the word count may vary a lot, but 80,000 words is probably a good target.

Women's Fiction
This is probably the most slippery and unhelpfully named of the genres. Like romance, it does tend to be written by and read by women, but it does *not* mean "all fiction written by women"! It's usually defined as a story about a woman's emotional growth or journey, and families or friendships usually play a big role. 80,000—90,000 words.

Memoir
I'm not specifically addressing memoirs in this book, but most of the guidelines in this book can probably be applied to memoir writing. 80,000 to 90,000 words is a good average length for this nonfiction genre.

Which genre are you writing? Maybe you knew this already. If you still don't know, take your best guess...or choose a genre that appeals to you and explore it.

KNOW YOUR GENRE

Now that you have an idea of your primary genre, you need to get to know it better.

Writers often ask questions like, "Can I have swear words in a young adult novel?" or "Can I have three first-person points of view in a thriller?" It's true that you can know a lot about a genre and still be unsure if a particular element will be accepted by agents, publishers, or readers. However, I often see questions that betray a basic lack of knowledge about the genre.

If you're a voracious reader of your own genre, then you probably have a good idea of the breadth of work that's been published in the past few years. But if you read all kinds of books, or if you haven't been doing a lot of reading lately, then you don't have a comprehensive understanding of your category, the way its biggest fans do. And that's a liability.

Some people will say they don't want to read books in their own genre because they don't want to be influenced by them. They think this will ensure their work will be different and original. This is exactly wrong. If you don't read in your own genre, you probably won't know if your plot has become a cliché and will need some kind of spin to make it fresh.

Even though you need to know your genre, I'm not going to tell you to read fifty books and come back next year. Instead, I'm going to give you a much easier assignment.

Read fifty product descriptions of best-selling books in your genre.
I'm talking about the description of the story that appears on the back cover of a book or in the description of a book that's being sold online. I think the easiest way to do this assignment is to get on a large website that sells books and go through best-selling books in your category. It may be hard to do this at a library because you only want to look at books that came out in the past few years, and a library will have books from different decades all mixed together on the shelves. You can do it in a large bookstore, but it may take a while.

However you do it, read fifty product descriptions. Keep a tally to make sure you hit your number.

You may be thinking, "Fifty? That's crazy. That's too many." But of all the advice I've ever given, this exercise is the one that people thank me for the most! It'll open your eyes to new possibilities and make you aware of plots that are played out.

More than that, it'll give you a stronger sense of how to sell a story. If you want to get traditionally published, you'll eventually be pitching your story to agents or editors, and if you want to self-publish, you're probably going to have to write one of these blurbs yourself.

Just do it. Study fifty product descriptions in your genre. As you're reading, you might want to make notes to yourself about your observations.

If you're undecided about your genre, read twenty-five apiece in two genres that interest you. This exercise alone might help you choose the one that's right for you.

ADDRESS YOUR CONCERNS

After you've done this exercise, you might be asking yourself:

What if people make fun of my genre?
Romance is the most maligned genre in fiction, hands down, but other genres have their detractors as well. Writers of horror, fantasy, science fiction, or young adult fiction may also hear, "Why can't you write serious fiction?"

And if writers are, in fact, writing serious fiction, people may insult that, too. "Why can't you write something more entertaining? You know, something that actually makes money?"

People are free to say whatever they want about your project. You are free to ignore them. You don't have to get mad. You don't have to take it to heart. You don't have to care one little bit. Your reaction is completely up to you.

Anyway, if you're going to be a writer, you'll need to be tough about criticism and rejection. Not caring whether people approve of your genre is a great place to start.

As a matter of professional courtesy, I recommend not maligning another writer's genre. If you haven't read many books in the genre, you don't know what you're talking about anyway. Every genre contains good books and bad books, and what makes a book good or bad is often a matter of personal taste.

Here's another question many writers have about genre:

What's the hottest genre...the easiest one to make money at right now?
If you can crank out a competent novel in a few months' time, then it might make sense to write in whatever genre seems "hot" at the moment. Otherwise, this is a losing strategy, because publishing trends can change quickly. By the time you finish your book, you may very well find that it's no longer the "hot" genre at all. In fact, by that time, it might be the last thing agents and publishers want.

There's nothing wrong with wanting to make money with your writing, but writing is rarely a successful get-rich-quick scheme. For most people, it takes a lot of time. If all you want is more money, you'd probably be better off moonlighting at a second part-time job.

The best genre for you to write in is one you love. It may be that you can write well in a few different genres, but true enthusiasm is hard to fake, and if you're not excited about writing something, your readers are unlikely to be excited about reading it.

Now let's address concerns about how your concept fits within your genre. Here's one I hear all the time, and you may have it after reading fifty blurbs.

What if my story is too much like someone else's?
Newer writers, in particular, worry about this way more than they need to.

When J.K. Rowling was writing Harry Potter, there were already a number of young adult fantasy novels telling the story of a boy who goes to wizarding school. Ursula K. LeGuin's *Earthsea* trilogy was one famous example. Rowling hasn't been the last to succeed with this basic storyline, either.

In a similar vein (heh), the huge popularity of the TV series *Buffy the Vampire Slayer*, not to mention the existence of L.J. Smith's young adult series *The Vampire Diaries*, didn't deter Stephenie Meyer from writing her *Twilight* series. And in fact, all of these stories owed a big debt to Anne Rice's novel *Interview With the Vampire*.

Some myths are deeply rooted in our collective unconscious. Magical weapons, resurrection, demons, fairies or "little people," changelings, ghosts, heroic quests, and other elements show up in stories across the globe.

Certainly, shared stories pervade people's cultural consciousness. The Norse sagas, Greek mythology, Arthurian legend, and the Bible, to name a few, have all had a huge impact on Western storytelling.

Beyond our shared mythological heritage, some human stories never fail to fascinate, terrify, inspire, or save us. That's why they come out in our writing and why we respond to them in other people's stories. Willa Cather said, "There are only two or three human stories, and they go on repeating themselves as fiercely as if they had never happened before." Given all that, if you encounter a story that's truly, eerily similar to your own, there's no cause to despair. Just do some thinking about how yours is going to be different. In fact, do some thinking about how yours is going to be *better*.

Look inside your heart and bring out more of those elements and those things that you need to say that will make your story truly your own.

After the blurb-reading exercise, though, you might have the opposite concern.

What if my story is too weird for my genre?
There are two possibilities here, and one is that you've gotten your genre completely wrong. If you thought you were writing a mystery, for instance, but the murder doesn't happen until the midpoint of the story and it's not crucial to the plot, you might realize you're writing something else.

If you have a story in mind that truly is unusual for its genre, you need to ask yourself if you believe it's a satisfying story and not *just* something you latched onto because it was so different. It should engage your heart as well as your brain.

If you think your concept will only attract a small audience, it's fine to decide you want to do something with broader appeal. It's also fine to write the best story you can for a small audience. It's up to you. And who knows? Your "niche" story may wind up having much more widespread appeal than you ever dreamed.

READ YOUR GENRE

When you were reading through fifty blurbs, did a few of the novels intrigue you? Great! Your other assignment for step 2 is to read a book in your genre. If you're still not sure what your genre is, read two books in two genres that interest you.

Even if you read books in a particular genre all the time, you may not read them with an analytical mind. As you read the book of your choice, *take notes*. Your notes can cover things like…

Did the first chapter get you hooked? Why or why not?

Did the main characters feel like real people to you? Why or why not?

What scene did you like the best? Why?

What scene didn't work for you? Why?

Write down sentences and lines of dialogue you particularly like.

I hope that after all this reading, your brain is buzzing with ideas. Whether that's the case or not, you have a better idea of where you may fit in publishing. Nice work!

CHECKLIST FOR STEP 2

- [ ] I know what genre I'm going to write in…or at least, I know I'm interested in a couple of genres.

- [ ] I've read 50 blurbs from best-selling books in my genre (or in two genres), which has given me a good understanding of what's already out there.

- [ ] I've addressed my concerns about my genre and how my story (if I already have one in mind) fits within it.

- [ ] I've read a book in my genre (or two books in genres that interest me), taking notes about what seems to be working and what isn't.

STEP 3: CREATE YOUR VISION

"So, what's your novel about?"

Writers don't always have a good answer to this question. Sometimes, they stumble over their words, or start rambling without managing to give a clear answer.

After you finish Step 3, I predict you'll be able to answer this question with panache. You'll say,

"Well, it's called (title of your novel here), and it's about (very quick description of your novel here.)"

Much more importantly, you'll have a clear vision in your head of the book you want to write.

In the past, you may have never had this. If you've finished novels before, you may have had tortuous rewrites as you figured out just what kind of book it was supposed to be. And if you've never finished a novel before, you may have struggled precisely because you didn't have this vision.

IF YOU'RE TRULY STARTING FROM SCRATCH

Most people reading this book will have at least some idea of the story they want to write. (Heck, some of them will have about a dozen ideas for stories they want to write.) Some people reading this will already have a few scenes written. If that's the case with you, you can skip over this section.

But what if you're truly starting with a blank page—with no earthly clue of what you're going to write about? No worries. You can figure it out.

Here are a few ways to find your story.

Goal + Conflict
Here's the simplest way in the world to write a story. Have a character want something…and put something in their way.

He wants to win an election…but he's caught up in a scandal.

She wants to go to college…but her family has no money.

He's innocent, but false evidence incriminates him.

She wants to have a happy home life…but she just found out her husband's been having an affair.

She wants to get back to modern times…and she doesn't even know how she got stuck in the Renaissance period in the first place.

He wants a dog, but his parents have said no.

He's a firefighter, and the wildfire is out of control.

She's a spy, and she's in grave danger of getting caught.

They want to get married, but their families hate one another.

On a basic level, stories *are* conflict. In books, movies, and TV shows, we see characters deal with everything from family squabbles to natural disasters, and we see them grow and change to meet new challenges. If you need extra inspiration, check out my blog post entitled "50 Character Goals (With Character Motivation)!"

Use Master Plots

There are many resources out there for very basic storylines. You can find many of them on my blog, bryndonovan.com (search "plots"), or in my books *5,000 Writing Prompts* and *Master Lists for Writers*. You can find other books and online sources for master plots as well.

Beginning with a master plot or writing prompt is *not* cheating. People like me who create and share writing prompts do it in order to inspire other writers and other stories. Right from the start, you'll be filling in the details about the characters, the setting, and the issues at hand. The way you develop the characters and the story will make it your own.

Take Inspiration From Other Writers

If you made lists of ten favorite movies and ten favorite TV shows in Step 2, go back and look at those again. What's happening in those stories? Would you like to write about a similar thing, but in a whole new way?

What are your favorite books? What are the main conflicts in them? Is that a type of conflict you'd like to start with to write a very different kind of novel?

It's not ethical to steal actual writing; nor is it ethical to steal the whole structure of a copyrighted work, plot point by plot point. Theft will get you in legal trouble, and rightfully so.

However, it's fine to get inspired by one basic element or one type of character you admire in another story. If you read a story about a family road trip gone wrong, for instance, and it inspires you to write a completely different story about a honeymoon cruise gone wrong, that's fine.

COME UP WITH A WORKING TITLE

Now you're going to figure out a title for your book. You can always change it later.

Having a title in mind can help you finish your story. If you're in the middle of a draft and feeling like you don't know what you're doing (a fairly common experience for writers in the middle of a draft), it's a lot more motivating to think, "Well, I better work on my women's fiction novel, *The Peach Pie Chronicles*," than it is to think, "Well, I better go work on that godawful mess."

With your finished novel, your title will be very important. It'll be one of the first things agents, publishers, and/or readers will know about your book, and it'll be a big factor in them deciding whether or not they want to read it.

You've probably noticed that the majority of bestselling novels have short titles: one to four words. Short titles are easier to remember, easier to refer to in marketing, and easier to work with when designing a book cover. Of course, there are exceptions, but you may want to consider something short.

If your book is the first in a series, you'll have not only a book title but also a series title. Avoid a third layer; it gets too confusing. For instance, if you name your fantasy novel *The Cinnabar Mage: Book I, The Wayfarer Trilogy: The Curse of the Conqueror* series, your readers are going to get lost.

If you have trouble coming up with catchy titles, here are three different formulas you might like to try.

Title Formula #1: Scream the Genre

This formula is all about making the book's genre very clear. It says to potential readers, "Hi! You know those stories you really love? This is one of those!" Conveying this message, through the title and/or the cover design, can make a big difference in sales. This particular approach may not be workable for mainstream or literary fiction, but for other genres, it's great.

Here's the basic idea for this title formula:

Choose a word that signals your genre in a clear way. Then add another word or a few words to round it out.

If you're writing fantasy, words like "dragons," "sword," and "queen" can signal your genre. For romance, "heart," "kiss," or "wedding" might do this. For a murder mystery, "death" or "murder" might be part of the title. Are you writing a work of historical fiction? Think about nouns that evoke the time and place of your story, such as "colony" or "patriot" for your American Revolutionary War saga.

Title Formula #2: The Open Loop

Some titles create a sense of mystery and arouse the reader's curiosity. The copywriter term for this is an "open loop."

Internet advertising uses the open loop all the time…because it works. Many people see a headline like, "You'll never believe this will help you lose weight," and even if they're full of skepticism, they can't help but click to find out what "this" is.

"Open loop" titles are a natural for mysteries, suspense, and thrillers, but they can work for several other genres as well.

Here are some examples of open loop titles.

The Lost Symbol by Dan Brown…what is the symbol, and why was it lost?

The Thirteenth Tale, by Diane Setterfield…first of all, what were the other twelve tales?

The Perks of Being a Wallflower, by Stephen Chbosky…what are the perks?

The Things They Carried, by Tim O'Brien…what things?

Everything I Never Told You, by Celeste Ng…what didn't she tell us?

Confessions of a Shopaholic, by Sophie Kinsella…what did she do?

Title Formula #3: That Familiar Phrase

Many novels take their titles from phrases in poetry or other works in the public domain. The phrase may be vaguely familiar to the reader... and even if it isn't, it has a nice, lyrical sound.

Chinua Achebe's classic novel *Things Fall Apart* takes its title from a line in the poem "The Second Coming" by W.B. Yeats. F. Scott Fitzgerald used a line from the poem "Ode to a Nightingale" by John Keats for his novel *Tender Is the Night*.

Aldous Huxley's *Brave New World* got its title from a line in Shakespeare's play *The Tempest*. William Faulkner's title *The Sound and the Fury* was inspired by a line from *Macbeth*.

Other book titles use common expressions and axioms, such as *Play It As It Lays* by Joan Didion or *'Til Death Do Us Part* by Amanda Quick.

Finally, many novel titles were song titles first. Song titles aren't protected by copyright, which is why there are titles like *As Time Goes By* by Mary Higgins Clark and *Norwegian Wood* by Haruki Murakami. A song title can evoke a strong mood for the story.

Title Formula #4: Focus on the Character or Characters

Many books are named after their main characters, directly or indirectly. *Bridget Jones's Diary* by Helen Fielding. *A Gentleman in Moscow* by Amor Towles. *Little Women* by Louisa May Alcott. *The Magicians* by Lev Grossman. *The Girl On the Train* by Paula Hawkins. *Martin Chuzzlewit* by Charles Dickens. *Eleanor Oliphant Is Completely Fine* by Gail Honeyman. *The Assassin's Apprentice* by Robin Hobb...you get the idea.

Take some time to try out different titles. Practice saying them out loud: "My novel? It's called..." Find something that rolls off the tongue.

ESTIMATE YOUR WORD COUNT

You're going to make a guess here about how long your novel will be. The finished first draft may be much longer or shorter, and that's fine! But the estimate will help you figure out how to stay on pace when you're writing your rough draft.

Most novelists use a common font and size, such as Times New

Roman, 12 point, double spaced. Still, novel length is measured in word count, not page length.

Some writers will say, in lofty tones, "A novel is exactly as long as it needs to be." That's in no way helpful to someone trying to understand what publishers and readers expect.

Established authors may release very long books, but it's much more difficult for a debut author to sell a very long novel. A manuscript that's much, much shorter than the requested length is also likely to get an automatic rejection. If you tell agents in your query letter, "I know it's short, but I can flesh it out if you want me to," that's not likely to help. They get many queries every day, and they don't have time to read your whole novel and think about how it could be made longer. They will likely expect you to get it into a form they can sell to publishers before you send it to them.

Even if you plan to self-publish, length matters. If your novel is over 100,000 words and you're not a well-known author, it'll be hard to sell it in paperback. You'll have to charge quite a bit in order to make a profit, and readers who don't know you well won't want to plunk down that much cash. If your story is very short, you won't be able to charge much for it—and on some retail platforms, you have a much lower royalty rate if your price doesn't meet a certain threshold.

In Step 2, I gave some average word counts for various genres. You should probably set a target that's typical for novel lengths in your category.

If you're truly in doubt, here's some unambiguous practical advice: start with 80,000 words as a target. It's a nice, average length that's comfortable for many publishers and many readers.

WRITE A SHORT DESCRIPTION

This may not be easy, but frankly, most parts of writing aren't. You're going to write a one- or two-sentence description of what your story is about.

Screenwriters call this the logline, and if you do an online search for sample screenplay loglines, you'll find lots of great examples.

Here are my short descriptions of a few famous novels.

A boy fakes his own death, runs away from home, and teams up with another runaway for adventure. (*The Adventures of Huckleberry Finn*, Mark Twain)

A woman only realizes she's in love with her good friend after another woman falls in love with him. (*Emma*, Jane Austen)

Three ghostly visitors make a man realize what a worthless jerk he is. (*A Christmas Carol*, Charles Dickens)

THREE COMMON STORY ISSUES

Here are three common problems that writing a short description can reveal.

1. Not enough is happening.
For example, consider this description:

A girl struggles with mental illness, and her family doesn't understand her.

It sounds like the end of the book will be the same as the beginning. No thanks. Your novel is like a train, and most people are going to be mad if they expect a journey and they wind up just circling the depot instead.

Now what if things change for this girl over the course of the story?

> *A girl struggles with mental illness, and her family doesn't understand her...but among the misfits in the psych ward, she finds friends and hope for the future.*

Is that too heartwarming for you? How about:

> *A young patient at a psychiatric hospital uncovers a horrific secret. But who's going to believe a schizophrenic teenaged girl?*

There are all kinds of possibilities! The point is, an issue or a state of being, all by itself, does not comprise a plot.

The other problem you may have with your description is...

2. Too much is happening.
If there is way too much story to describe in a couple of sentences without copious uses of semicolons and dashes, you probably need to focus.

You may be trying to fit six novels into the space of one. You don't need to do that! You can always write another novel.

Alternately, you may not be sure which is your main plot and which are the subplots, and you'll have to figure that out.

Here's the third issue you may uncover, and it's one I've struggled with before. (I've struggled with all of them, to be honest.)

3. There's not enough conflict.
Let's say your storyline is:

> *A veterinarian and a dog owner fall in love.*

As a romance reader and a dog lover, I'm interested! But what obstacles does their love face? If they don't have any issues, it's not going to be an interesting read.

But let's say it's more like:

> *A shy veterinarian and a cynical lawyer with a doting hound dog can't deny their feelings for one another.*

Okay, I can at least see how his shyness and her cynicism will be impediments. Whatever your story is, make sure that the short description includes a hint of conflict.

Let's say you've fussed with your title and your short description for a while. You've got something that's okay, but you know it's not great.

What do you do? Do you keep messing with it until it's fantastic? It's up to you, but I'd say no. Don't spend too much time here! If you're trying to take one step a week, for instance, make the story idea as good as you can this week and move on. This step is for you, and it doesn't have to be perfect to give you some clarity and focus.

GET EXCITED!

Now you have a title and a short description of your novel, as well as the genre and a very rough target for length.

This is great!

In the weeks and months to come, if someone asks you, "So, what's your novel about?" you're not going to stammer and stumble. You'll casually say something like,

"It's a thriller about a high-society wife in Manhattan who's actually a Russian spy, but her husband's on to her. It's called *Sofia in Soho*."

They're going to be so impressed!

Here are two other things you can do to get motivated to write. They're both optional, but they're a lot of fun.

Design a Fake Book Cover
Now, let me be very clear: this is probably just for you. Months from now, if you're querying agents, you don't want to send along a cover you designed yourself. That's a way to tell an agent, "I'm a total amateur."

And if you're planning to self-publish, then ideally, you'll want a professional-looking cover. Unless you're an experienced and talented designer, you're probably not going to be able to pull it off.

Nonetheless, a fake book cover design can help you feel like your project is real. Creating one is a great exercise for thinking about your story and the kind of experience you want to create for readers.

If you don't know how to use Photoshop, then go to Canva.com. They make it easy to design a book cover. They even have a special template and sample layouts.

If you intend to share it publicly—on your blog, Facebook author page, and so on—then you need to use truly copyright-free images or else get the rights for them (pay a stock photo site for them, for instance.) Canva.com does include lots of free images, as well as ones you can purchase for a dollar.

Whether you keep your fake book cover design on your computer or print it out and hang it on the wall over your desk, it can be incredibly motivating. You'll have a vision of your finished goal: your completed, published novel.

Make a Playlist

Every time I start a new novel, I create a playlist of songs for it. The very act of choosing songs for the playlist focuses my imagination on the story. Sometimes, I even get an idea for a line of dialogue or a scene!

When I'm writing, the music keeps me in the right mindset for the story. If I've had a stressful day of work or if I have other personal problems weighing on my mind, hearing my novel playlist again can clear away my worries and snap me right back into the world of the story.

I have no trouble writing while listening to songs with lyrics, but most people prefer instrumental music when they write. Movie and videogame scores are great material for writing playlists—especially if you haven't seen the movie or played the videogame, so you don't have any specific associations with it. But all kinds of classical, jazz, new age, and other instrumental music can work. Just find music that fits the overall mood of your novel.

Congratulations on discovering a clear vision for your book!

CHECKLIST FOR STEP 3

- [ ] I have a working title for my novel.
- [ ] I have a short description of my novel.
- [ ] I have a very rough word count target for my novel.
- [ ] I'm excited about writing it.

STEP 4: CHOOSE YOUR POINT OF VIEW AND MEET YOUR CHARACTERS

I'VE OFTEN HEARD PEOPLE TALK about plot-driven versus character-driven stories, or ask the question: "Should I start with the characters or the plot?"

This is a false dichotomy. Your plot should be related to your characters' goals, the ways they react to things, and the way they change, grow, and learn over the course of the story.

Does a main character have to change or learn from the beginning of the novel to the end? Not necessarily…but if he or she doesn't, it'll be that much harder to create a story that satisfies readers. Some villains or antagonists, though, never learn anything.

MAKE DECISIONS ABOUT POINT OF VIEW

Is This Going to Be in First Person or Third Person?

You can write in a character's point of view in the first person or the third person. The first person uses "I" and "my," and sounds as if the point of view character is telling the story. It's like this:

> I sprinted after her, the hot pavement searing the soles of my feet.

The third person uses pronoun "he" or "she," like this:

> He sprinted after her, the hot pavement searing the soles of his feet.

Second person—"you go here, you do that"—is rare, and can come off as gimmicky. However, there are some successful novels written in second person, such as *The Fifth Season* by N.K. Jemisin and *Bright Lights, Big City* by Jay McInerney. If you're going to write in second person, I strongly recommend reading at least a couple of good examples.

Novels in the third person most often switch from one character's point of view to another. Most novels in the first person stick with one character's point of view all the way through.

A small percentage of first person novels switch off between two or even more characters. This structure can be successful if each point of view character has a unique voice and style. The alternating first person points of view won't be as engaging if the chapters all sound alike.

If you choose third person, you can still convey the character's innermost thoughts and feelings. (To read more about deep point of view, see Step 16.)

I don't know why, but newer writers are always asking if they can switch between first person and third person in the same novel. You can do whatever you want, but few novels are written this way, it may lower your chances of getting a publishing contract, and it may confuse or annoy readers. At the very least, you should be able to articulate a clear reason for the choice.

How are you going to decide between first person and third person? You might simply have a preference for one or the other. You might choose first person because you love the unique voice of your main character. Or you might choose third person because it's more typical for your genre and you want to have multiple points of view without switching off between first person voices.

Who Are My Point-of-View Characters?

Some novels are written in omniscient point of view. The story is told by a narrator who sees everything and knows everything. Omniscient point of view was much more common in the 19th century than it is today, but you can still find a few contemporary novels that use it.

More typically, though, contemporary novels use *point of view characters*. For a whole scene, a whole chapter, or a whole book, you're in one character's head. If you're writing from the point of view of a teenage girl, for instance, you only see what she sees, and you only know what she knows. You're privy to her thoughts and sensations—and only hers.

Your point of view characters are your main characters. They're the star of the show. If your book got made into a movie, they're the ones who would be on a movie poster.

How Many Point-of-View Characters Are Too Many?

One of the most common mistakes newer writers make is having too many point-of-view characters. I've seen so many people wind up unable to finish their novels because they were juggling too many characters.

Even if you are able to finish it, if you have five or more different point of view characters, it's going to be more of a challenge to write a story that readers will enjoy. They'll have a hard time making a strong connection with all of them. They might even have trouble keeping them straight.

Readers frequently enjoy a secondary character who doesn't have an arc, but it's hard for them to stay interested in a point of view character who doesn't have an arc. An *arc* is the way a character grows and changes throughout the story. The new recruit becomes a seasoned warrior. The bitter loner becomes a villain mastermind. It's hard enough to figure out one or two character arcs and make them work with the story…let alone six or eight.

With a lot of point-of-view characters, your readers may get impatient and start flipping pages, waiting for you to get back to the one or two characters they really care about…the ones you should've made the main characters in the first place, instead of part of an ensemble.

You'll also have the challenge of giving multiple point of view characters more or less equal time. Oh, and you'll need to alternate between them fairly regularly, because if one of them disappears for half the book, that's going to feel weird. That can be very difficult when you're also trying to move the plot along at a satisfying pace.

If you've never completed a novel before, I strongly recommend sticking to one or two point-of-view characters rather than adding these layers of complexity to your work.

But, hey—it's your novel.

WHAT IS HEAD-HOPPING, AND WHY SHOULDN'T I DO IT?

Head-hopping is something that typically happens in stories written in third person. The writer bounces back and forth between the thoughts of one character and another within a scene. Head-hopping looks like this:

> Josiah froze behind the bar of the saloon as Emmeline strode in, pistol in hand. Hatred burned in her eyes because she'd heard that he burned down the barn. Holy mackerel, Bob thought, and stopped playing the piano. Emmeline took aim at Josiah's heart. Would he try to come up with some excuse? She wasn't even going to wait to find out.

The more generally acceptable way would be to pick one person's point of view and stick with it. Here's the whole scene rewritten so that we only have access to Josiah's perceptions.

> Josiah froze behind the bar of the saloon as Emmeline strode in, pistol in hand. Hatred burned in her eyes. *Oh, no*. She'd heard that he burned down the barn. The piano music stopped. Emmeline took aim at his heart, now pounding wildly in his chest. Would she even give him a chance to explain?

Head-hopping doesn't refer to alternating points of view. If a scene from Josiah's perspective is followed up by a scene from Emmeline's point of view, that's fine. It refers to flipping back and forth without warning within a scene.

Some authors stay in one point of view for a whole chapter, which keeps things very clean. Others allow themselves to switch when they start a new scene.

It's all right to switch a point of view *once* in the middle of a scene (though I wouldn't do it often). To indicate a point of view switch, leave an extra space between the two paragraphs.

Whenever you switch from one point of view to another, you want to make the switch clear in the first sentence or two of the new point of view.

Staying in the point of view of one character for a while means that you're not just telling your readers a story. You're allowing them to really *experience* it, through the thoughts and the perceptions of a character.

This helps them get completely lost in the story. It also makes them bond with your characters more strongly. Both of these things will make them love you as an author, and that's what you want.

What's the Difference Between Head-Hopping and Omniscient Point of View?
Honestly, this can be tricky, but novels written in omniscient point of view have a distinctive voice or writing style that remains consistent throughout the story. The narrator feels like another character—someone who's telling you the whole story.

DEVELOP YOUR MAIN CHARACTERS

Now that you know who will be your main characters, it's time to learn more about them.

1. Name Your Main Characters
One of the first things we learn about people when we meet them are their names. It's also one of the first things readers learn about your novel. It's important to get the names right.

Where do you find names?
If your character lives in the United States, go to the "popular baby names" portion of the government's social security website. You can put in the year of your character's birth and then pull up the top 1000 baby names for that year. You're likely to find something you like! Then do an online search for the top 1000 most common last names in the United States.

If your character lives in a different country, you can mix or match names you find in the news or on social media. Naturally, if you're writing historical fiction, you'll need to do your research to make sure you're choosing appropriate names.

Here are a few pieces of advice for character naming.

Use consistent logic for imaginary names.
If you're writing a fantasy or science fiction novel, you may be inventing names. The trick here is to make sure names that all belong to the same culture or civilization have a similar feel. If you have two fairy sisters, one named Glitterwing and one named Carol, that's going to feel weird.

Use names that readers will know how to pronounce...unless there's a good reason not to.
Most readers dislike stopping to puzzle out a name or mumbling over it in their head every time it appears in the story. Some writers include a glossary of pronunciations in the back of the book, but most readers won't want to work that hard. However, there may be some historical periods and some settings in which you need to use hard-to-pronounce names in order to stay true to your story.

Avoid weird names.
I don't mean less common names. I mean ones that make the reader wonder what the heck your character's mom was thinking. It's actually kind of a cliché for a character to explain his bizarre name to other people in the book.

If you're using an unusual first name, it's often a good idea to ground it with a simple last name. A great example of this is Indiana Jones.

Make sure your characters' names aren't too similar to one another.
If all of your characters' names begin with the same letter, your reader is likely to get them mixed up.

2. Learn More About Your Main Characters

There are a lot of character worksheets out there, online and in books. If you like personality typing systems, you might use Myers-Briggs types or the Enneagram to help figure out your characters. I have a series on my blog, bryndonovan.com, about using zodiac signs to help develop characters (and you don't have to believe in astrology at all to find it useful).

While you don't want to put a real person in your fiction, you might have elements of a character inspired by someone you know.

To help you get to know your characters, I do have one exercise for you: play Twenty Questions. Ask your character all of these things and write down what they say. You might be surprised at what they tell you!

1. How old are you?

2. Describe yourself physically.

3. What's a typical, everyday outfit for you?

4. Describe your living situation: who do you live with, and what's your home like?

5. What was your childhood like?

6. Who are the three people you're closest to now—family members, friends, someone else?

7. How would the people who know you best describe your personality?

8. What are your talents?

9. How do you make a living—or do you?

10. What do you do in your free time?

11. Tell me about a fantastic thing that happened to you once.

12. Tell me about a terrible thing that happened to you once.

13. When was the last time you were angry, and how did you react?

14. What's something that terrifies you?

15. What are your religious or spiritual beliefs?

16. What are your bad habits or addictions?

17. How do you usually act in social situations with a lot of people?

18. What are five things you love and five things you can't stand?

19. If you could make one dream come true, what would it be?

20. What do you think might keep that dream from ever coming true?

If you like this kind of thing, you could also look up Dr. Arthur Aron's 36 Questions "that make you fall in love with anyone," and ask your character those…or you can come up with questions of your own. No matter which questions you choose, asking your characters about important things and writing down the answers will give you a pretty good sense of who they are. Even if you thought you knew them, you might learn a couple of new things in this interview.

Do this for your point of view characters and also for your villain, if you have one, whether he or she is a point of view character or not.

Thinking About Character Dynamics

This is a great time to think about how your point of view characters will react and respond to one another. Answer some of these questions for yourself.

1. What will they admire about each other, if anything?

2. What will they have in common?

3. What will they find strange or surprising about one another?

4. What will they disagree about?

5. Will they react differently to good news? How?

6. Will they react differently in a crisis? How?

3. Figure Out Your Main Characters' Arcs

I mentioned earlier in this chapter that a character arc is the way the character grows, learns, or changes over the course of the story, in response to their experiences. Here are a few more examples of character arcs:

A true believer in a cause becomes disaffected. She walks away…or even turns traitor.

An arrogant man learns he needs to get help and advice from others to reach his goal.

A workaholic realizes she's wasting her life and stops spending so much time at the office.

Someone who was cynical about love comes to believe in it again.

An ex-warrior heals from post-traumatic stress disorder.

A son becomes more understanding and forgives his father.

A wife finds the strength to leave her abusive husband.

This is going to be hard, because you may discover more about your characters' arcs over the course of the story. But for now, at least make a guess about your characters' arcs.

For each point of view character, write down a sentence about how they will grow, change, or learn over the course of the story.

Good job on getting to know your characters better! This will make your plot more interesting and believable…and it'll make your story easier to write.

CHECKLIST FOR STEP 4

- [ ] I've made a decision about whether to write in first person or third person point of view (or second person point of view, although this author doesn't particularly recommend it).
- [ ] I know who my point of view characters are.
- [ ] I've named my point of view characters.
- [ ] I've asked each of my main characters at least 20 questions, and I've written down their answers.
- [ ] I've written down a sentence or two to describe the arc of each main character.

STEP 5: PLOT YOUR NOVEL

Some people hate plotting. They often call themselves "pantsers," because they write by the seat of their pants. Many people who hate to plot ahead say that they want to be able to discover things along the way.

Well, guess what: when you plot ahead of time, you still discover things along the way! They might be small and delightful things, or they might change your plot significantly.

A plot is a road map. A road map doesn't keep you from getting caught in a thunderstorm or taking a side trip. It just keeps you from running out of gas in the middle of nowhere, with no cell phone service, wondering why you even left home.

Many newer novel writers have trouble making things actually *happen*. But things have to happen for your story to be interesting. That's one of the reasons why I encourage you to figure out some important events ahead of time.

If you can't stand plotting and you think it's not your style, that's fine…*if it works for you*. If you've completed a few novels without doing any plotting and they were successful, then clearly, you don't need to plot ahead.

But if you've never plotted ahead and you've dabbled at writing for a few years, starting several novels and never finishing any of them…or maybe finishing one or two that are so messy, you're not sure where to start with the edits…it's time to face facts. Your process isn't working for you. It's not leading to success.

They say "insanity is doing the same thing over and over again and expecting different results," but I don't think that's insanity. It's human nature. Writers often won't even consider changing their process, and then they wonder why they can't get ahead. They blame their lack of talent, when in fact, they have plenty of talent. It's their resistance to change that's to blame.

To improve your progress, improve your process. This applies to so many things.

If you're still not convinced to plot ahead, consider this. Writers who get multi-book deals don't always have the book two and book three in the series written. They often have a completed book one and only the plot for books two and three. If you're interested in writing a trilogy or a series, knowing how to plot could benefit you immensely.

Successful authors often get book deals based on the synopsis before they've even written the story. In my day job, that's how I make most book deals with authors. If you intend to be a bestselling author, you might as well figure out how to plot now.

And here's the last reason why I think you should plot first. You can get feedback from a beta reader on the plot outline before you even begin writing. Your beta reader may alert you to a plot hole or logic problem that's easy to fix in an outline. If you become aware of a plot hole or other issue in a completed manuscript, you may be cutting one hundred pages and writing two hundred more. It'll be painful and incredibly time-consuming. I'm trying to spare you that.

Even if you start out as someone who thinks making an outline isn't your style, you may wind up being terrific at it. You may even come to love it.

You've Already Started Plotting

You realize this, right? In Step 3, you wrote a short description of your story. Step 4, you wrote a sentence or two about the main characters' arcs—the way they change, learn, or grow throughout the story. You already have the skeleton of a plot.

So let's flesh it out!

THE INDEX CARD METHOD...FOR PEOPLE WHO HATE PLOTTING

Let me introduce you to my bare-bones method for people who really, really don't want to plan ahead...and who only have one or two main characters. If you're the kind of writer who creates fascinating characters, writes vivid descriptions, and crafts beautiful sentences, but you struggle with making things actually *happen*, you are not alone...and this index card is going to be a game changer.

All you need is a 5 x 7 index card. (Or probably about ten of them, since you might cross things out and start over.) You can actually use this method for a story with more than two main characters, but you're not going to have enough room to write, so you'll need to use a piece of paper instead.

Make horizontal lines dividing the card into seven rows. They don't have to be equal. Whatever.

Here's what your index card would look like for two characters.

main character 1	main character 2
inciting incident	inciting incident
big thing happens, 1/4 in	big thing happens, 1/4 in
bigger thing happens, midpoint	bigger thing happens, midpoint
huge thing happens! 3/4 in	huge thing happens! 3/4 in
OH NO, CRISIS! near the end!	OH NO, CRISIS! near the end
THE BIG FINISH	THE BIG FINISH

Row One
Write your characters' names in that first row.

Row Two
Write down what's called the *inciting incident* for each of the characters. In case you're not sure what that is, I'll explain.

The inciting incident is the event that kicks the story into motion. In *The Wizard of Oz*, the inciting incident is the tornado that drops Dorothy and Toto in the Land of Oz. In *Pride and Prejudice*, it's Elizabeth's first encounter with Darcy at the ball.

Although the inciting incident is more often something that happens to a main character, it can also be an action that the main character chooses to take. For instance, the main character goes to a job interview, kills a slave owner, or asks someone to marry them.

This incident is going to come pretty early in your novel. A friend of mine who teaches improv tells her students, "Start on the day everything changes." You may have some setup before your inciting incident—or you might hook your reader with it in the first sentence.

Here's how you fill out the rest of your index card.

Row Three

For each character, write down **something big that happens.** This could be about 1/4 of the way into your story.

The big things that happen might be the same for both of your main characters, or they might be different. Make sure these events are turning points for your characters: places where they make important decisions and/or take significant actions. As the story goes on, they may be doing things they never dreamed of doing.

I know you don't have a lot of room in these boxes. That's good! That'll force you to keep things simple, like this:

- He asks her out.
- She steals the necklace.
- He takes a train to St. Louis.
- She gets the job.

Row Four

For each character, write down **the second, bigger thing that happens.** This could be about halfway into your story.

We've all read a lot of books that dragged in the middle. That's not going to happen in your story, because you've got something exciting happening right here.

Row Five

Write down **a huge thing that happens,** around 3/4 of the way into your story.

Row Six

Here it is, between the 3/4 point and the end: the bleak moment. The crisis. Everything looks hopeless. All is lost!

Of course, the hopelessness depends on the genre. In an action adventure novel, the bad guys might be torturing the hero. In a romantic comedy, the two people may have broken up, and one of them might be listening to old songs and sniffling.

Row Seven

Write down **the end.**

Your characters take their most dramatic actions yet, and we see the consequences. Could be good. Could be bad. It's your choice. Great story!

Now, people who are accustomed to intricate, serious plotting may roll their eyes at my Index Card Method. But if you use it, keeping in mind that those big events are turning points for your characters, it'll force you to do some thinking about character goals, motivation, and development. You'll figure out all kinds of other issues as you write, but you've got your key events and your escalating conflict, so your reader will become more and more engrossed as they read.

OTHER PLANNING METHODS

Some people prefer to write out a two- or three-page synopsis of the story. For authors who plan to submit their finished novel to agents or publishers, there's a big advantage with this method. You're going to need a synopsis in order to submit, and writing a synopsis of a finished novel is difficult. It's much easier to write it ahead of time, even if you have to make changes to it later.

Even if you don't want to write a whole synopsis at this point, you can try a short version. Imagine your book is already for sale. Write the back cover copy, or the blurb—the description of the book you'd see on a bookseller's or publisher's website. This will probably be anywhere between seventy-five to one-hundred-and-fifty words, although it's fine if it goes longer, since it's just for you right now.

For another approach to plotting, check out the book *How to Write a Novel Using the Snowflake Method*, by Randy Ingermanson. This has worked for many people who are averse to plotting and don't think in a linear fashion.

THREE THINGS TO ASK YOURSELF ABOUT YOUR PLOT

In my experience as an editor, plots often fall flat for one of two reasons: motivation and character arc. To save yourself the anguish of writing an entire novel with a fatal flaw like this, ask yourself these two things now.

1. Is there a conflict?
Remember: without a conflict, or a problem or obstacle of some kind, you don't have much of a story.

2. Do my main characters' actions and decisions make sense?
Your main characters typically need to have understandable motivations for doing the things they do. Often, these motivations will be common sense. If your main character's house catches on fire, he'll grab his cat and run outside, and then call the fire department. While he's waiting, he might try to put out the fire himself with a garden hose, if he can do that without endangering himself or Fluffy. Those are reasonable actions to take.

If your character is in a situation where there are several reasonable courses of action, you may need to eliminate a few. For instance, let's say your character is poor, so she robs a bank. Well, your readers will be able to think of several more reasonable ways to address the issue of poverty. Many of them aren't going to be on her side. They may not even be able to stick with the story.

But what if she's living during the Great Depression, when hardly any jobs exist? And she doesn't have a shot at the few jobs that do exist, because they're seen as men's work? And a man who cheated her husband out of his life savings, leading him to die of a broken heart, happens to own a big bank? *Well.* Now we're on to something. She's got every reason to rob that bank, and the readers will cheer her on.

If there's anything in your plot that would make a reader think, "Why didn't he just do X instead?" then you need to address that.

The more unusual or irrational your characters' actions are, the stronger their internal motivations need to be. Their actions need to be consistent with their past, their hopes for the future, and their personality.

3. Do My Main Characters Have Arcs?
In many fantasy stories, the hero goes from a nobody to a skilled warrior who defeats an evil overlord or empire. It's a familiar tale, but not one I'm going to get sick of in my lifetime, as long as it's handled well.

What if someone wrote a story about someone who started out skilled and defeated an evil overlord or empire? You'd think that would be a stronger idea, right? It's more realistic, and it's less clichéd!

But if you write that story, you're going to have to show the character growing or changing in some other way, or else I'm not going to be that interested.

And lots of readers feel the same way. We like to see people improve and adapt in order to overcome obstacles. Maybe even as we're being entertained, we learn valuable lessons (or at least get reminders) of how we can triumph in the face of adversity in our own lives.

In my day job, I pass on projects all the time because there's an arc for one main character, but not for the other. For instance, I'll get romance novels where the heroine has to overcome some obstacle in order to let herself fall in love with the hero, but the hero is smitten with her from the first time they meet. It's much more interesting if both characters develop over the course of the story.

Optional: Type It Up
You're going to share your plot outline with a beta reader or a friend or two whose judgment you trust. If it isn't typed already, do that now, unless you have very neat handwriting. If you used the index card method, you probably don't need to type it.

CHECKLIST FOR STEP 5

- [ ] I've written a synopsis or at least a basic outline for my story.
- [ ] If it's on the computer, I've backed it up somewhere so I won't lose it.

STEP 6: GET FEEDBACK ON YOUR PLOT

IN THIS STEP, YOU'RE GOING to share your basic plot with one or more people and get their opinion on it.

These shouldn't be just any people. They should be people who want you to succeed. While they don't have to be writers themselves, they should have intelligent opinions about stories. They should be people you trust and respect.

Why are you doing this? So that if there's a weakness in the story or something that doesn't make sense, you can pinpoint it now.

If you wrote a complete draft of your novel and then realized it had a fatal plot hole, you might wind up throwing away a hundred pages and writing a hundred new pages. This might cost you several months and a piece of your soul. You might just give up on the whole thing.

If your spouse, your friend, or that person in your writing group points out a fatal plot hole in your outline, you won't enjoy it. Depending on your temperament and how you feel about the story, realizing there's a problem may make you feel frustrated or embarrassed. But then you can take a couple of days – or even a couple of hours – to fix it. It's much better to catch it now.

Ask the Right Questions

If you're getting a critique from someone who's experienced in critiquing stories, you may be able to ask them, "Do you think this plot is working?"

If it's someone whose judgment and intelligence you trust, but they're not accustomed to critiquing plots, you can ask them questions like this.

- *Do the characters' actions make sense to you?*

- Did you wonder why the character didn't do something else instead?
- Do any plot points seem implausible? (Even if it's a fantasy or science fiction story, the plot points should seem believable within the world of the story.)
- Do you have any questions about the plot?
- Does anything feel wrong, off, or dumb to you?
- What do you like best about this story idea?

WAYS OF GETTING FEEDBACK

1. *By email.*
You might email your outline to someone if they live far away from you or if there's some other reason why you can't get together in person to discuss it. In this scenario, you'll need to give the other person (or people) a couple of days to read and respond. Depending on location and schedules, you might get together with this person to listen to their feedback or they might email it to you.

Do establish a firm deadline. Two or three days should be enough time to read an outline and get back to you. If they're late in giving you feedback, it's okay to politely prod them. Yes, they're doing it for free, but once a person agrees to do something, it's their responsibility to follow through.

That being said, it can be difficult to get people to find the time to read and comment on something. When someone agrees to give feedback on writing and then doesn't follow through, it can be disheartening. You might be tempted to think, "Well, I guess my story idea is terrible then." A non-response usually has to do with forgetfulness, poor time management skills, a lack of commitment, or a mixture of all the above. It usually has nothing to do with the quality of the writing.

Because it can be hard to pin people down to give you feedback, you might want to ask a few or several people.

2. *In a one-on-one meeting.*

This can be nerve-wracking for an introverted writer, but it can also be more effective. Get together for a Zoom meeting, meal, coffee, or drinks with the person giving you feedback. If you have a very short and simple outline – such as the index card in the last step – you won't even need to let them pre-read your outline before discussing it. You can show it to them, walk them through your story ideas, and ask them for their opinion.

3. Online.

If you're in an online writing group, you can post your plot outline and ask for feedback. Some writers won't want to do this because they'll worry about their ideas being stolen, even though that's a very rare occurrence. A bigger concern is whether you feel like all of the people in the group will sincerely want to help you and have your best interests at heart. I only recommend this route if there are at least several people you trust and respect in the group.

RECHARGING AND RENEWING

If you're emailing your plot outline to someone, you're going to have a little down time while you're waiting for their response. And if you've gotten feedback from someone, you may want to take a day or two to digest and consider it.

Waiting for feedback and processing feedback can both be stressful experiences for writers. Even if this kind of thing doesn't make you anxious, this is a great time to recharge your brain and take care of yourself. Inspiration and self-care are both so important to the process of writing.

Read

Distract yourself by reading another book in your genre. Heck, there may be something in the book you choose that inspires you to make your plot better.

As an alternative, you can read a book for research. If you're writing historical fiction, science fiction, or about anything you don't have firsthand knowledge with—from art authentication to firefighting—then use this time to learn more.

Of course, if you're writing fantasy, you might want to use this time for more world-building.

Refresh

This is important. For most people, it's a lot of work to write on top of going to school, going to a day job, parenting, running a household, and other responsibilities.

So treat yourself for getting this far with a refreshing experience. An experience is the best reward because it can also inspire your creativity.

Here are a few examples…

Pop some popcorn and watch a movie.

Take a walk in the park or the woods.

Visit a museum (many have virtual tours online).

Give yourself a manicure and pedicure.

Play a board game with your partner or family.

Work on a craft project.

ACCEPTING AND EVALUATING FEEDBACK

When you get feedback from your beta readers, your job is to consider it and see if it can help you make your plot stronger.

What If I Don't Agree With Other People's Input?

Let's say that you got some feedback that sounded weird and wrong. And in spite of that, you kept an open mind and considered it. And it's been a few days and you're still sure they're totally off.

That's fine. It's your story, and you're free to ignore what someone tells you. There's no reason to be angry at the person who was wrong, either. Chances are they were trying to help, and nobody's perfect.

If you don't agree with the feedback you get—or if someone shrugs and tells you, "It looks good, I guess," instead of giving you anything you can use—you'll have to try again with someone else.

What If Getting Critiqued Hurts My Soul?

If you're fairly new to receiving constructive criticism, you may find it difficult. It's human nature to want approval, and many people who don't even require much in the way of others' validation feel a deep need for it when it comes to their creative work.

Whenever we're trying to do something difficult and time-consuming, the encouragement of friends and family can make all the difference. It's fine to ask someone close to you for encouragement and praise at any stage in the writing process.

But when you're asking people for critique, that's something totally different. Your beta readers are working for you—usually for free—to make your story better. You're not working for them. You don't need their approval. You need advice you can use.

When you get that advice—the very thing you asked for—you may feel embarrassed because you want your beta readers to think you're smart and talented. But who cares if they do or not? They're only a few people.

You may be annoyed that you didn't see the problem yourself. Don't even worry about that. It's hard to see flaws in one's own work. This is why we have beta readers and why editing is a profession.

CHECKLIST FOR STEP 6

☐ I've gotten useful feedback on my plot outline from one or more people I trust.

☐ I've read another book in my genre.

☐ I've treated myself to an experience of creative renewal.

STEP 7: FINESSE YOUR PLOT

In this step, you're going to use the feedback you got on your plot outline to make it better. This might be a tweak or a major overhaul.

I can't give much advice here, because every story is different. I will say in my experience, most plots are fixable. It may not seem that way at first, but if you brainstorm possibilities, you're likely to come up with the answer.

I do have one piece of advice if you're struggling.

Let's say someone's pointed out a gaping plot hole. The hole may seem bigger than the rest of the story—a black hole even, sucking everything else in. It may seem hopeless, and you may feel completely discouraged.

One thing I like to do in this situation is tell my subconscious to work on it. And yes, I do this out loud. Like this:

> "Hey, subconscious, could you please figure out how to fix the problem with the bank heist? And can you do it in a couple of days? Thanks."

Then I don't think about it for a couple of days. And guess what? My subconscious serves up the answer, right on schedule. This has never failed me, and it might work for you, too.

But if you really can't fix it, the worst-case scenario is that you start over with a new story idea—and you've only burned a few weeks instead of a year or two writing the whole draft. So you can't feel too badly about that. Maybe you were just getting warmed up.

You have a huge imagination, with thousands of stories inside you… whole constellations of them. You can always work on another story.

Once your outline or synopsis is complete, you might like to print it out and post it over your writing desk, if you have one—maybe right next to the fake cover of your novel. Or you can just save it to your computer's desktop where it's in easy reach.

CHECKLIST FOR STEP 7

☐ I have a revised synopsis or basic outline for my story.

☐ I've backed up my work so far.

Congratulations!
Congratulations on finishing Section I of this book…and prepping and plotting your novel. If you've gotten impatient and you've written some scenes already, that's great! Those scenes we write quickly, in a rush of inspiration, are often some of the best and juiciest scenes in a book.

And if you've never done preparation and advance plotting for a novel before, you should feel especially proud. While writing is never easy, working some of this out in advance is going to make the writing process so much smoother.

SECTION II: WRITING THE FIRST DRAFT

STEP 8: WRITE CHAPTER ONE

IT'S TIME TO JUMP IN and write your first chapter.

Don't worry about making it perfect – that's what the entire third section of this book is for! Worry about getting it *done*.

THREE DOCUMENTS TO START USING NOW

Here are three Word documents that can help you as you create your first draft. If you're writing your first draft longhand, these might be three folders instead.

The Bits and Pieces

Short snippets of dialogue, random descriptions, and other fragments may pop into your mind as you're writing your draft. The stuff that comes spontaneously into your head is often great material – but you may not even know where it goes yet.

Don't lose it! Keep it all together in a document called "Bits and Pieces." (Since I don't always have my computer with me, I often write snippets like this down in my planner or my phone and transfer it to this document later.)

The Outtakes

Let's say you cut a short exchange between characters, or even a whole scene...and then later, you regret it. You'll have to write it all over again. So annoying, and such a waste of time! If you keep all your deleted material in a document, it's there for you in case you change your mind. (Once the book is published, some of your fans might be interested in deleted scenes!)

The Fix List
When you're writing a first draft, issues and changes will occur to you as you go. You can keep going back again and again to change things, but sometimes that can kill your momentum. On the other hand, you don't want to forget about them.

If you keep a document called "Fix List," you can use it to keep track of all the things you need to change. Once your first draft is done, you can go back and address all those issues.

ALWAYS BACK UP YOUR WORK!

If I could only give one piece of advice to writers, it would be this:

Back up your work.

Maybe you've never known the pain of losing a huge amount of writing. I have, and it's excruciating.

Remember, it's not a question of *if* technology will fail you, but *when*. Your computer could get destroyed or stolen. Email your work to yourself after each session or use a cloud solution—whatever works for you. You can also save it on USB drives, but they can get lost or damaged, so don't make this your *only* method.

If you're working in Word, prevent smaller losses by making the program auto-save more often. Go into Preferences, choose Save, and adjust it so it saves your work every one or two minutes.

How Do I Format a Novel?
When you're finished with this work, what will the document you send to an agent or editor look like? You don't have to put it in that form yet—but then again, you might choose to, in order to make things easier on yourself later.

A novel manuscript should be one single Word document, rather than a bunch of documents, one for each chapter.

Create a title page with the title, your name as the author, and the word count (actual or rounded to the nearest hundred—as you like.) Put contact information in the bottom righthand corner—phone number and email are the most important elements.

Use a simple, readable font in a reasonable font size (Times New Roman, point size 12, is typical.)

Set 1" margins all around.

Double space! It makes it easier for beta readers, agents, and editors to make notes, and it's easier on their eyes.

Number the pages.

Chapter headings start on a new page.

You can indicate section breaks with a centered hashtag symbol.

What the First Three Pages Should Do

However you begin your story, remember that you don't want a bunch of backstory in Chapter One: here's where the character grew up, here's what her family is like, and so on.

Your mission in the first three pages is simple:

Convince readers to keep reading.

One of the best ways to do this is to get readers to care about what happens to the main character.

This doesn't necessarily mean readers have to *like* the main character. However, fiction does have many more likable than unlikable protagonists. Some readers only like books if the main character is easy to root for. Writing a likable character is a lot harder than it looks. Writing an unpleasant character that keeps an audience riveted may be even more difficult.

One way or another, in those first three pages, you want to hook the reader and get them interested in what happens next.

How *Not* to Start a Novel?

I've read many warnings against starting a novel in the following ways. However, you shoul keep in mind that writing doesn't have any hard-and-fast rules.

- *A description of the landscape or the weather.*

Lots of good novels actually open this way. As a reader, it doesn't bother me at all, unless it goes on for too long.

- *"My name is…"*

This is, basically, the famous opening of Herman Melville's *Moby Dick* — "Call me Ishmael." It's also how *Never Let Me Go* by Kazuo

Ishiguro begins. Oh, and *Everything Is Illuminated* by Jonathan Safran Foer. And *Gateway*, the sci-fi classic by Frederik Pohl.

It may be overdone, though.

- *A dream.*

Yes, this is a cliché. On the other hand, Donna Tartt's *The Goldfinch*, a fantastic and entertaining novel that won the Pulitzer, begins in this way: "While I was still in Amsterdam, I dreamed about my mother for the first time in years." Daphne du Maurier's classic *Rebecca* opens like this: "Last night I dreamt I went to Manderley again." I think it helps in these cases that you know it's a dream. The authors aren't jerking you around.

- *An alarm clock buzzing/waking up.*

This isn't in any books that I like, as far as I can recall. I'd avoid it unless you have an absolutely brilliant reason for doing it.

THIRTY WAYS TO START A NOVEL

But if you're still not sure about your beginning, it might help to look at ways your fellow authors have started *their* novels. I'm a huge believer in the inspirational power of lists, and reading through the list may spark a new or better approach to your own story.

1. The arrival of a letter, email, or package. (*The Thirteenth Tale*, Diane Setterfield.)

    This could be momentous. However, it could simply tell the reader about the character's everyday life, such as a distasteful private message on a dating site.

2. A main character in a frustrating situation.

    This can also give your readers a feel for her everyday life, while making them empathize with her right away. Maybe her car has broken down, or her cat is puking.

3. A main character in an awkward or embarrassing situation.

Maybe her cat is puking on the lap of a visitor she was trying to impress.

4. The discovery of a dead body.

    This is a popular beginning, and not just for murder mysteries.

5. The death of somebody in the family or the community. (*All the Pretty Horses*, Cormac McCarthy; *The Known World*, Edward P. Jones.)

    This is also a popular one, and understandably so, because an ending is a new beginning.

6. The beginning of a disaster. (*All the Light We Cannot See*, Anthony Doerr.)

    It could be a bombing, a plane crash, a fire, or a tornado.

7. The aftermath of a disaster or calamity. (*Their Eyes Were Watching God*, Zora Neale Hurston; *Little Fires Everywhere*, Celeste Ng.)

8. A kiss.

9. A performance, or the conclusion of one. (*Bel Canto*, Ann Patchett. This opening also includes a kiss!)

10. A main character in the hospital. (*Kindred*, Octavia Butler.)

11. A main character declaring that he is in big trouble. (*The Martian*, Andy Weir.)

12. A main character who's clearly in big trouble. (*What Is the What*, Dave Eggers.)

    She might be getting mugged or running from soldiers.

13. The arrival of a plane, ship, or train. (*The Count of Monte Cristo*, Alexander Dumas.)

The character might be on board, or she might be watching it come in.

14. A scene at a party, a bar, or a nightclub. (*War and Peace*, Leo Tolstoy; *The Name of the Wind*, Patrick Rothfuss.)

15. A fight. (*Children of Blood and Bone,* Tomi Adeyemi.)

    The character may be participating in the fight or witnessing it.

16. A character moving in to a new place.

    It could be a neighborhood or a dorm room.

17. A broad statement about one's life. (*One for the Money*, Janet Evanovich.)

    One for the Money begins, "There are some men who enter a woman's life and screw it up forever. Joseph Morelli did this to me—not forever, but periodically."

18. A dramatic moment in the middle or end of the story. (*The Secret History*, Donna Tartt.)

    You can begin here and then backtrack to explain how they got there.

19. A trial in a courtroom. (*Snow Falling on Cedars*, David Guterson; also an example of #18.)

    A milder version of this: your character faces a judge or judges in the form of a parent, a manager, or peers.

20. A job interview.

    I like this idea because you could get a lot of information across about your character naturally. She might be giving appropriate answers while her internal monologue tells you the rest of the story. Also, an applicant at a job interview is in a vulnerable position, which would create empathy for your heroine right away.

21. A main character meets someone new. (*Wuthering Heights*, Emily Brontë; *The Big Sleep*, Raymond Chandler.)

A stray cat? A future lover? Someone important, probably.

22. A street scene. (*Perdido Street Station*, China Miéville.)

Your character could be getting an errand done or going to visit somebody. For a novel that takes place in an historical, futuristic, or fantasy setting, this can be a good way to establish a sense of place as well as establish your character's normal life and priorities.

23. A main character in a triumphant situation.

You might be setting her up before you knock her down. She could be giving a speech, winning a race, or accepting an award. It could also be a smaller personal triumph, such as successfully fixing a car or turning in her term paper on time.

24. A character or characters getting dressed, shaving, putting makeup on, or doing their hair. (*The Makioka Sisters*, Junichiro Tanizaki.)

25. A big, happy occasion such as a wedding or a graduation.

Of course, it might or might not be happy for your main character, who may be a participant or someone in the audience.

26. One character teaching another how to do something.

This is another way to establish your main character's personality and his everyday life. If he's a father, he could be teaching his son to hunt or to cook rice properly. If he's an insurance salesperson, he could be giving the new guy some tips.

27. A character or characters discussing something worrisome. (*Return of the Soldier*, Rebecca West.)

28. A main character coming across a significant object.

    It could be a photograph of a lover she intended to forget or a strange relic that turns out to be magical.

29. A character committing or apparently committing a crime. (*Beartown*, Frederik Bachman.)

    She might be the main character, or she might be the antagonist.

30. A character or characters doing a job. (*Our Mutual Friend*, Charles Dickens; *Fahrenheit 451*, Ray Bradbury.)

    This could be an unusual or startling job, or a more ordinary one with emotional significance. For writers who struggle with getting their characters to *do* things, this might be a good option.

WHAT ABOUT A PROLOGUE?

If you want to write a prologue, well, I can't stop you, and some prologues work well in novels. A lot of them don't, which is why some readers skip them and why many agents and editors (I am one of them) dislike them.

If the prologue is just a way to provide the reader with a bunch of backstory or introduce the reader to the world of the novel, it's almost always better to weave that into the story here and there. If nothing's happening, it's going to get boring fast.

Prologues that are fully fleshed out scenes that take place several years before the present-day narrative—but feature one of the main characters—are usually more likely to make the reader care what happens next.

HOW LONG SHOULD MY CHAPTERS BE?

There are no hard-and-fast rules here, and it's going to vary depending on the type of story you're writing. If it's a fast-paced thriller, your chapters may be shorter, and if it's a richly detailed historical novel with an epic sweep, your chapters may be longer.

If your chapter is shorter than 2,000 words, ask yourself if there's a good reason for it being so short, and if it's over 6,000 words, ask yourself if there's a good reason for it running so long.

Short chapters can feel choppy unless they end in such a way that makes readers feel like they *have* to keep on reading. Readers feel a sense of accomplishment when they read the end of a chapter, so when the chapters are too long, they may feel frustrated or feel like the pace is dragging (which may or may not actually be the case).

You might decide to break some of your chapters differently once you revise the novel, but for now, make your best guess at what Chapter One ought to be.

CHECKLIST FOR STEP 8

- [ ] I've started three other documents: Bits and Pieces, Outtakes, and Fix List.
- [ ] I've figured out a way to back up my work after every writing session.
- [ ] I've written Chapter One.
- [ ] I've backed up all my work so far in case my computer gets destroyed.

STEP 9: WRITE CHAPTER TWO

Right now, you may have the urge to rewrite Chapter One. Obviously, you can if you want. You can rewrite it seventeen times, if you so choose. But I'm going to encourage you to move on and write Chapter Two. If there are things you want to change about Chapter One, make a note of them on your Fix List.

If Chapter One was all in one character's point of view and you're going to use more than one point of view, you might want to switch here if it makes sense for the story.

If you didn't have the inciting incident in Chapter One, you should probably have the inciting incident by the end of Chapter Two. If you're struggling to get there, you may be laying more groundwork or including more backstory than is necessary.

Because you're introducing characters in these opening chapters, let's talk about describing characters' physical appearances.

DO YOU HAVE TO DESCRIBE HOW CHARACTERS LOOK?

Usually, it's a good idea. As writers, most of us want to create characters that feel like real, flesh-and-blood people to readers. One way to do this is to help readers picture the characters in their imaginations.

A character's clothing choices can also give the readers early hints about what the character is like. In some cases, you might have fun with subverting their expectations (maybe the middle-aged woman in the tacky sweater is actually a trained assassin).

You don't need a whole paragraph or more early on about your character's looks. In fact, unless you can figure out a clever and natural way to set it up, it's better to avoid this. You might have a sentence or two describing them when they first show up. As a scene plays out, you can mention things like, "Tia ran a hand through her long brown hair," or "The crinkles around his eyes deepened as he grinned."

HOW TO DESCRIBE A CHARACTER'S LOOKS IN THEIR POINT OF VIEW

This can be tricky. Since people don't usually go around thinking about their physical appearance, how can you convey to your readers what a point of view character looks like?

Maybe Don't Do This: The Mirror Scene.
Lots of books in first person have a scene near the beginning that goes kind of like this:

"As I brushed my teeth at the sink that was a little too short for my six-three height, my reflection stared back at me—olive complexion, angular face, square jaw. My brown eyes still looked bleary, and my short black hair—already flecked with silver, at the age of thirty-five—was sticking up on top. I dug around for a razor and shaved, which made the cleft in my chin more obvious…"

Honestly, I think a quick line of description as the character looks in the mirror is fine, but a long paragraph in front of the mirror is a bit tedious and overdone.

Have your character imagine what other people are thinking—or not thinking—about their appearance.
"She probably hadn't expected to have a fifty-year-old bald guy like me in her freshman composition class."

"The guards would never notice me: a slim twenty-year-old woman in a regulation uniform, blending in with all the other space academy students heading home for winter break."

If you take this approach, though, I recommend avoiding what I call the Insecurity Litany. Writers do this more often with female characters, and it reads kind of like this:

"As I walked up to the witness stand, I regretted choosing the red dress—it only called attention to how plump I was. With my prominent nose, I'd never been exactly pretty. At least I have long blond hair—my best feature—and I'd curled it that morning so it spilled over my shoulders. I'd taken extra care with my makeup, but my lipstick couldn't do much for my narrow lips..."

If I read a passage like this, I think, *You're about to testify, and you're thinking about this? Really?* Unless a preoccupation with her appearance is an important part of her personality, this approach doesn't make a lot of sense.

Here are some other ways to describe your characters' looks in their own points of view.

Try using incidental movements.
- "I adjusted my glasses."
- "I pulled my long hair back into a ponytail."

Show what they can and can't do.
- If she's short, she might look someone in the eye—but have to look up to do it.
- If she's tall, maybe another character asks her to get something off a high shelf.
- If he's a big guy, he might have trouble squeezing into an airline seat.

Show how other people react to them...
- "His gaze traveled along my curves."
- "Her eyes widened as she saw the scar on my cheek."
- "He asked if he could help with my bags, and I shook my head. Even though I was eighty-five and five-foot-nothing, I wasn't nearly as frail as I looked."

And have other characters comment on or react to their appearance.
- "You have your father's hazel eyes."
- "That green dress looks good with your red hair."

Have your character respond to the weather.
- "My pale freckled arms were beginning to burn in the blazing sun."

- "Thanks to the humidity, my hair was bigger and frizzier than ever."

Give yourself a pat on the back, because you're not just thinking about or talking about writing a novel...you're really doing it!

CHECKLIST FOR STEP 9

- ☐ I've written Chapter Two.
- ☐ I've written the inciting incident in either this chapter or Chapter One.
- ☐ I've included at least a little physical description of my characters.
- ☐ I've backed up all my work so far, because all computers fail at some point.

STEP 10: WRITE CHAPTER THREE

Welcome to Chapter Three! If you've gotten this far, you have a solid start. I'm going to address a couple of common writing issues, and as always, skim over them if they aren't helpful to you.

HOW TO FORMAT DIALOGUE

Most fiction writers set off lines of dialogue with quotation marks, like this.

"The words that the character actually says go inside the quotation marks," he said.
Tanya nodded. "That makes sense."
"I don't think it does," I said.

Now, let me point out a couple of things in the above example.

The first character's line of dialogue ends with a comma. Any time you have a dialogue tag right after the line of dialogue—*she said, Luis retorted*, and so on—the period at the end changes to a comma. An article like *the*, *a*, or *an*, or a pronoun like *he, she, we*, or *they*, is lowercase in this instance. *I* remains uppercase.

If the line of dialogue ends with a question mark or an exclamation point, it doesn't get changed into a comma if a dialogue tag comes after it. The pronoun remains lowercase.

"It's confusing, isn't it?" the teacher asked.
"Yes!" we all yelled.

Let's look back at this line.

Tanya nodded. "That makes sense."

Even though there's no *Tanya said*, we know it was Tanya saying this, because she nodded first. Here are a few more examples of action tags like this.

The old man frowned. "Well, that's one solution."
She tossed the shovel in the back of the truck. "As long as nobody digs it up again."

Setting some lines of dialogue up like this will improve your writing. You won't be repeating "said" too often and your readers will be better able to imagine the characters, which will make them stay more grounded in the scene.

Here are a few other questions I've been asked about dialogue.

Do I indent every line of dialogue?
A line of dialogue from a new speaker begins a new paragraph—even if it's a one-sentence paragraph. New paragraphs are indented, like this:

The captain gulped down the last of his rum and set the cup down on the wooden table with a clank. "Bring me my sword."
"You're too drunk to fight," the pirate said.

If the same character continues speaking, you don't need to start a new paragraph. For instance:

"Bring me my sword," the captain said. *He took the last gulp of his rum and banged his tin cup down on the table.* "By God, I'm going to challenge that octopus to a duel."

Should I try to use a lot of synonyms for 'said'?
No. Synonyms like *commanded, stated,* and *explained* are fine here and there, but "said" is the right choice most of the time…unless it's a question, in which case, "asked" is the right choice most of the time.

If you constantly use synonyms for *said* and *asked*, you'll slow down the flow of your story. The synonyms tend to call unnecessary attention to themselves.

It's easy to avoid repeating *said*. Use action tags like I explained, and remember that if two people are talking, you can go back and forth between them a couple of times without any kind of tag. Take a look at lines four and five in this example.

"Do you want to go to the beach?" he asked her.
"I don't know. The traffic will be bad."
"Yeah, we should've gotten up before noon."
She stiffened. "Hey, wait a minute. Isn't our wedding today?"

When do I write "said Bryn" and when do I write "Bryn said"?
The term for the first one is an "inverted dialogue tag." In older novels, these were common, but they've fallen out of favor in contemporary fiction. If you stick to the second way of doing it, you may save a copyeditor a lot of time down the road.

How Do I End a Chapter?
Do you ever hear readers say, "I couldn't put this book down"? The way you end the chapters can help readers devour your book faster…and love it more.

Not every chapter needs to end on a dire cliffhanger. Honestly, that could get exhausting and lose its impact. But there are ways to create tension instead of ending a chapter with the feeling that everything's settled. They include:

- a character has an important realization
- a character asks himself – or someone else – a question
- someone asks the main character a question
- something big is revealed
- a character is about to reveal something big
- a new character is introduced

- two point-of-view characters the reader knows meet each other
- a character is about to do something big or scary
- a character's just gotten into trouble

And so on. If you don't nail it in the first draft every time, that's no big deal. You can always change chapter breaks in the revision process.

CHECKLIST FOR STEP 10

☐ I've written Chapter Three.

☐ I've formatted dialogue properly and have included some action tags.

☐ I've thought about how to have a good ending sentence to the chapter, even if I haven't gotten it exactly right yet.

☐ I've backed up all my work so far in case my computer crashes.

STEP 11: FIRST BETA READING

Take a deep breath, newer writers: it's time to plunge in and get some other people's feedback on your writing so far.

If you've never done this before, your hands may shake as you turn over your chapters—or press *Send*. Even if you're used to getting feedback, you might still feel some jitters if you're working on a different type of story than you've ever done before.

You may be asking yourself: shouldn't I wait to get feedback until I'm done with the first draft?

Writers are always telling each other, "Don't edit now! Just keep writing! Finish it first!" But if there's a fundamental problem with a character, or if you keep falling into the same bad writing habit again and again, you want to address that now. Otherwise, your revision process later will be overwhelming.

Here's a question I hear a lot, though:

WHAT IF MY BETA READERS STEAL MY IDEAS?

Experienced authors rarely worry about this. Here's why.

Ideas are easy. Execution is hard.
Even if a premise is first-rate, a writer has to figure out thousands of little things to make it work. The expression "The devil is in the details" is all too true.

Most writers like their own ideas better than other writers' ideas.
It's common for a writer to have about ten or so fragmented ideas floating around in their own heads, waiting to be written. These stories

have personal significance to the writer, they've already taken root in the writer's subconscious, and someone else's idea has little chance of supplanting it.

Ideas are not copyrightable.
Actual writing can be copyrighted. Premises and ideas can't. For this reason, it's better for writers to focus on the writing rather than on protecting the concept.

Most ideas aren't that original, anyway.
We've covered this before, but someone has probably already written a storyline similar to yours. And that's fine! It's the way you handle it that will make yours unique.

QUESTIONS TO ASK YOUR BETA READERS

You're going to get the best quality feedback if you tell your beta readers exactly what you need. Send them three to five questions with your draft and add more as they come up

The questions are going to vary from project to project, but here are some sample things you might ask your critique partners.

- *After the first three pages, were you hooked? Why or why not?*
- *Did everything make sense to you? If not, what didn't?* (This open-ended question can reveal everything from confusing character motivations and unclear prose to continuity issues and big, gaping plot holes.)
- *Did you like the main characters? Why or why not?* (If you don't intend to write a likable protagonist, you can ask, *Were you interested in the main character?*)
- *What could be improved about the writing style?* (This is a great thing to ask now, because it can prevent carrying a mistake or unfortunate tendency throughout the rest of the draft.)

Whatever else you ask your beta readers, ask them this.

- *What did you like about the three chapters, and why?*

Writers need to hear what they are doing right, because they are often even more clueless about their strengths than they are about their weaknesses. A writer with a sense of humor or a natural gift for description may not give those things much thought, because those things came easily to them. But as a writer, you need to be aware of your strengths so you can build on them.

Have you ever loved a book even though you were all too aware of its shortcomings? That's because what the writer did well, they did *very* well.

In any sphere of your life, focusing only on what you're bad at is a terrible strategy and rarely leads to success. Becoming a good writer isn't just about fixing everything you're doing wrong. It's even more about playing to your strengths! So you depend on your beta readers to take the time to tell you what you're doing *right*.

SET A DEADLINE AND HOLD THEM TO IT

As I've said before, it can be very difficult to get feedback on your writing—even from people who have agreed to do it! If that's your experience, don't take it as a criticism of your writing. I've never talked to a writer who didn't struggle with this problem.

If you send someone your chapters electronically, ask them to confirm that they've received them and can open the document. Beyond that, give them a deadline, like you did before when you asked for feedback on your plot. One week is plenty of time to read and give feedback on three chapters—unless a beta reader is having an incredibly busy week.

If they don't get it back to you on the agreed date, contact them *the next day* to ask if they will get it to you soon. And don't be shy about politely nudging them another time after that if they say they'll get it to you soon and they don't. (Polite nudging is a valuable skill for all writers.)

CHECKLIST FOR STEP 11

- [ ] I've given my three chapters to beta readers for feedback.
- [ ] I've given them a deadline to get back to me.
- [ ] I've given them specific questions to answer, including "What did you like about the three chapters?"

STEP 12: CONSIDERING YOUR FEEDBACK

GIVE YOURSELF A FEW DAYS

Your beta readers have given you feedback on your first three chapters. They may have conveyed them in an email, in person, or in the form of margin notes. You've thanked them for their time and their thoughts—whether you actually feel grateful or not.

Now what?

Many of us tend to react too quickly to feedback and criticism. We think things like:

> "This story is terrible. I need to throw it away and start fresh."

> "This story is *really* terrible. I need to give up writing entirely!"

> "I'm going to change every single thing they told me to change, right now."

> "This person is completely wrong about my story. How dare they? It's fine as it is!"

Here's how I recommend handling feedback:

1. Read through all of it.
2. Set it aside and don't even think about it for a few days.

Instead, clean your house. Go on a hike. Go shoe shopping. Work on another writing project. Binge watch TV. Whatever you like.

When you come back to the feedback a few days later, you're not going to feel as emotional about it anymore, and your subconscious will have had time to mull it over and come to some conclusions.

You may realize, *Actually, I can address all of those things. It's fine.*

You may suddenly think: *Hey! There's a way to fix that seemingly impossible plot hole!*

You may decide: *You know what? I think they're wrong on that particular issue. I'm keeping it the way it is.*

RECOGNIZING AND DISREGARDING TOXIC BETA READERS

Even terrific, helpful, vital feedback can sting, particularly on a bad day. That's okay. We can handle a little pain and get past it. But not all beta readers are well-meaning.

If your critique partner isn't invested in your success, but rather invested in tearing you down (whether she's aware of this or not), she's not going to be good for you. She may be someone who seems like your friend, but in this situation at least, she is not.

Here are a few signs of a toxic beta reader.

A toxic beta reader conveys scorn in her comments.

She doesn't say, "This character could be more well-rounded." She says, "This character is flatter than the paper the story is printed on."

A toxic beta reader yells at you.

Exclamation marks, one or more. All capital letters, as though your writing is a dire emergency. (Calm down, Carol. Nobody ever died from an awkward sentence.)

A toxic beta reader never points out what you are doing right.

If you followed my instructions in Step 11, you specifically asked for what was working in the story. Some well-meaning people forget to do this…but some not-so-well-meaning people refuse to do it. Either way, if they neglected to give you positive feedback after you asked for it, they didn't do a good job.

A toxic beta reader suggests maybe you shouldn't write at all.

This person just disqualified herself from being someone you need to listen to about writing, or about anything else, ever.

Why are some beta readers toxic? There are probably a lot of reasons.

Some of the harshest people, and the loudest negative voices in workshops and writing groups are some of the least productive and accomplished. Sometimes instead of trying to raise themselves up, people try to tear others down. Toxic beta readers may use criticism as a substitution for creative work and bring the drama and the jokes that should go into their own stories into the feedback they give.

Successful writers can be toxic beta readers and community members too, though. (Honestly, I have no idea what their problem is.)

The friend you asked for feedback may be jealous of you. He may resent the fact that you are writing at all, because he's not doing anything creative himself.

Your beta reader may have a grudge against your story or genre. You're writing about a heroic soldier? She's a pacifist who hates the military. You write romance? He believes all romance novels are insipid. True, he's never read one in his life, but no matter; he's sure he's right. Besides, he thinks you're writing lies: his last relationship was a disaster.

As beta readers, we should try to be aware of emotional reactions that have nothing to do with the quality of the writing. I believe in honoring a commitment to give feedback. However, there are a few types of stories that would make me say, "I'm sorry, but I'm not a good audience for this."

How do you handle toxic beta readers? Say, "Thanks for your time!" Then never think about their mean-spirited comments again, and never ask them for their opinions again. Some mean people *want* to know they hurt your feelings. Don't give them the satisfaction. And more importantly, don't allow them the opportunity to do it again.

Of course, some beta readers may not be toxic, but inept. They tell you they loved everything, or they have suggestions that make no sense. Eh, well. Still thank them profusely, because they gave you their time and they tried.

(Okay, granted, a beta reader who says he loved everything may not have actually read your story at all. Thank him anyway. At least he's expressed good will.)

DON'T QUIT NOW

Of course, if you're feeling overwhelmed and discouraged, starting a new story is always an option. But if all you do is write the beginnings of stories, that's not going to get you to where you want to be—the author of a finished novel.

The messiest, worst drafts can become polished, terrific books. To get to your finished draft, you have to be willing to buckle down and do the hard part of revising.

Sometimes, edits that seem like they'll take forever go more quickly than you expect! So believe in the spark of inspiration that led you to the story in the first place.

MAKE A REVISION PLAN

If you dive in and try to fix everything, sentence by sentence, you may feel overwhelmed. Break it down. Make a list of everything you need to fix, and then fix each thing one at a time.

Here are a couple of examples of revision checklists to give you an idea of how this works.

Revision Plan, Prisoner of Winter, *Chapters 1 – 3*
- Add some description of the arctic fantasy landscape.
- Make it clear earlier that he's going to a penal colony.
- Cut some of the history of the penal colony (can weave some more in later maybe?)
- Cut most of the adverbs, especially relating to dialogue.
- Change his crime to something less evil so everyone doesn't hate him.

Revision Plan, Mermaid Summer, *Chapters 1 – 3*
- Try to make my main character sound more like a 15-year-old and less like an adult. Use YouTube and that one documentary for research.

- Cut the boring beginning where she's taking a math test and going to gym class.
- Explain why the mean girl invited her to the pool party.
- Make it more obvious that her legs become a tail.

Your revision plan will give you a clear way to move forward.

If you're still new to getting critiques, give yourself a little reward for having the courage to show it to someone. Give yourself another one for being brave enough to hear or read through the comments. You're doing what you need to do to learn your craft.

CHECKLIST FOR STEP 12

☐ I've thanked my beta readers.

☐ I've read over my beta reader feedback.

☐ I've let it marinate in the back of my mind for a few days.

☐ I've made a revision plan.

STEP 13: REWORKING CHAPTER ONE

In this step, you're going to apply your revision plan to your first chapter. It may take a while. It might even take as long as it did to write the first chapter! That's perfectly normal. Get out your playlist, make a pot of coffee or tea, and get to work.

DESCRIBING SETTINGS

Many writers add more description in revision. That's why I thought this would be a good time to talk about describing settings.

Writing descriptions of scenery and surroundings comes more naturally to some writers than others. If you're wondering why your novel is too short or moving too fast, that's sometimes due to a lack of character development or to the plot itself. Sometimes, though, it's caused by a lack of description, including descriptions of settings.

Here's what good descriptions of settings can do.

They help people get swept up into the story.
When people can imagine the surroundings of the story, their real-world surroundings fall away. One of the reasons people read is to escape to a different world.

Sometimes it's more pleasant—a charming small town, a glamorous big city, or a cottage on the beach—almost like a virtual vacation, for the low price of a book.

Sometimes it's fantastic—such as a futuristic moon colony, a fantasy realm, or Heaven — sparking readers' imaginations.

Sometimes it's difficult or even grim. This can make readers imagine how they would survive and conquer in similar circumstances, giving them a feeling of empowerment. Or it can make readers empathize with terrible situations they've never personally experienced.

They underscore the mood of the scene.
If you're writing a high-stakes boxing match, describing the spotlights, the size of the venue, and the roars of the crowd will get your readers' adrenaline pumping even more.

If you're writing a quiet scene on a front porch at night, the chirping of crickets and the flickers of fireflies will add to the peaceful ambience.

The setting can also make a scene more memorable by contrasting with the emotions of the scene. For instance, someone at a party gets terrible news, or someone who's in an empty building at a remote location finds a beautiful love letter tucked in his backpack.

Here are a few tips for describing settings.

Focus On a Few Details
Some writers balk at the idea of describing settings because they don't want to write long, boring passages. Good news: you don't have to. For each scene, just think of a few details that will convey the mood you're looking for.

For instance, let's say your character visits her grandma who's lived in the same tiny New York City apartment for fifty years. You might write about peeling paint on the walls, shelves full of framed photos and knickknacks, and the fact that the old-fashioned radiator heater makes the place too hot for your main character. There! Your reader already has a feel for the space.

Intersperse Details Here and There
This is another way to avoid going on and on. Instead of writing one big paragraph describing the setting, weave some of the details into the narrative. (You can do the same thing when you're describing people's looks.)

For instance, in the above example, your main character might notice the heat and the peeling paint on the walls right away. Then she might sit down on a floral sofa and notice the knickknacks and trinkets on the shelves. Later, her conversation with her grandma might be interrupted by the banging from the radiator.

Use Photographs and Videos
If you're having trouble visualizing a scene in your head, do online searches of similar settings for inspiration. To describe the sunrise in the opening of my novel *Sunrise Cabin*, for instance, I used a photo of a sunrise that I'd taken myself (even though Paige's sunrise was over the Colorado Rockies, not the Kansas City skyline.)

Revision is actually my favorite part of writing. In the first draft, I'm just producing the raw material—the clay. In subsequent drafts, I'm shaping and sculpting it into something special. I hope you find yourself enjoying the process, too—even if you didn't expect to.

CHECKLIST FOR STEP 13

- [ ] I've done my first revision of Chapter One.
- [ ] I've added a little description of setting if I didn't have any before.
- [ ] I've backed up my work so far in case my computer freaks out for some reason and loses it.

STEP 14: REWORKING CHAPTERS TWO AND THREE

Apply your revision plan to chapters two and three. Hopefully, these will go quicker than chapter one. The first chapter often takes the longest to rewrite because it lays so much groundwork for the rest of the story. Every project is different, though!

If you're like a lot of writers, you may have some questions about your characters or the content of your story. I'm always hearing writers ask:

IS IT OKAY FOR ME TO WRITE ABOUT THIS?

Writers can write about anything they want. It's not illegal unless it's slander or libel. So if you're asking yourself this, stop and think about what you *really* want to know. It might be something like:

"Will agents or publishers dismiss my story because of this?"
"Will readers get mad at me for writing this?"
"Am I a bad person for writing this?"

Here are a few of the specific things writers often ask.

Is it okay to write about a (Black, or transgender, or disabled) character, when I am (white, or cisgender, or able-bodied) myself?
If all of us only wrote characters who were the same as us, our fiction would be weird and boring. And because the world is filled with all

different kinds of people, populating a fictional world with people of only one gender, one race, one sexual orientation, and so on can feel unrealistic and exclusionary.

I've heard some white writers say, "I only include characters who aren't white if there's a reason for it in the story." This is nonsense. I ask white writers who say this: does a character need a reason to be white? No. So they don't need a reason to be Latina or of Asian descent, either.

I've also heard writers say, "I just don't say what race my characters are." White readers will almost always assume characters are white unless they're told otherwise. In fact, there have been a couple of notable instances in which white readers believed a character was white *even though the book said otherwise.*

When authors are writing outside of their own identity, they need to be very aware of stereotypes and harmful tropes so they can avoid them. They should do a lot of reading and research in order to try to get it right. It's also worth researching workshops and learning opportunities in order to do the best job they can.

I do think writers should realize that not all stories are theirs to tell. As a white writer, I'm not going to write a novel that centers on a Black character dealing with racism. As an able-bodied writer, I'm not going to write a novel about how a person comes to terms with her disability. I'm almost certain to get these stories wrong.

Authors writing outside of their own identity often hire and pay sensitivity readers. For instance, a Christian author writing a Muslim main character might pay a Muslim editor to read through their manuscript and make sure there's nothing offensive, embarrassingly inaccurate...or just off. Using a sensitivity reader is no guarantee that someone else won't criticize your work later, because no one person can represent the opinions of millions of people. However, it's still very helpful.

How disturbing is too disturbing?

If you're thinking about putting grim elements or shocking scenes in your story, you may wonder how far is too far. Two things can guide you here: genre expectations and intention.

If you're writing a horror novel or a gritty true crime tale, your readers are probably expecting some disturbing content. But in some genres, readers won't be expecting twisted scenes filled with gruesome details. If that's what they get, they're likely to be irritated, upset or disappointed.

You also want to be clear about your intentions. Why are you including the disturbing or shocking scene? If you simply have a desire to shock or upset readers, well, that's not a particularly noble motivation. If they respond with negative comments or reviews, you have no reason to complain: you were negative toward them first.

With violent content, it's good to be aware of overused tropes. Violence toward women, in particular, has been used over and over again as a way to motivate characters. It's best to avoid this unless you have something unique to express that can't be conveyed in another way.

But violence or gore, in judicious amounts, may serve the story. You might feel it's needed in order to make the subject matter realistic. It might make your readers' hearts bleed for the main character (who is literally bleeding) and get them emotionally wrapped up in his or her escape or recovery.

If you want readers to like your protagonist, there are limits to what kinds of acts they can commit. You're not required to write a likeable protagonist; however, some readers hate books with unlikeable ones, which may make these books a tougher sell to agents and publishers.

I'm writing some unflattering things about my family members. What if they get mad at me?
Let's be clear: if you do that, they probably *will* get mad at you. Here are some of your choices.

You can write a memoir or obviously autobiographical fiction and let the chips fall where they may. But to do this, you may have to be willing to destroy relationships.

You can write a very different kind of fictional novel, but draw upon those experiences. If you change all the details and the specifics, it can become something completely new, while still carrying the emotions and the messages you want to convey.

Or you can decide you're sick of thinking about your past and discard it as subject matter. Writing more hopeful stories might even be good for your mental health.

Of course, you might do all three of these things in the course of your writing life. You just need to make a decision for this particular book. Indecisiveness will hinder your progress and keep you from finishing your story.

Did you finish revising your first three chapters? Congratulations! This is an important milestone. A lot of readers make a decision about whether they like a story at around the three-chapter mark. Some agents and editors will ask for submission of a synopsis plus the first three chapters: if they like what they read, they'll ask to see the rest. You'll make more revisions to these chapters later, but it's great that you have a solid start.

CHECKLIST FOR STEP 14

- [ ] I've done my first revision of Chapters Two and Three.
- [ ] I've contemplated my relationship as an author to the content of my story.
- [ ] I've backed up my work so far in case my computer crashes.

STEP 15: WRITE TO THE MIDPOINT, PART I

Your story has a firm foundation. You've already worked out a lot of issues. Now, it's time to make serious progress. In the next six weeks (or the next six steps), you're going to get to the midpoint of your novel. You may be writing very quickly, depending on how long you expect your finished draft to be.

WRITER MATH

Hey, remember when you estimated the final word count of your draft? You're going to use that number now to figure out your word count goals for the next six weeks.

Take your estimated final word count, divide it in half, subtract the word count you have so far in your first three chapters, and then divide that number by six.

Now some of you may be thinking, "Bryn, I went into writing in order to *avoid* math." Don't worry. This is simple.

Let's say I'm writing a thriller, and I expect the final draft to come in at around 80,000 words. To get halfway done, I'd need 40,000 words. I look at what I've got already: 10,344 words.

40,000
10,344 -
29,656

That leaves me with 29,656 words to write in the next six weeks. If I divide that number by six:

29,656 / 6 = 4,943 (rounded up)

4,943 words a week for the next six weeks will get me to the midpoint of my novel. That's not bad at all. It's about 706 words a day.

Write your weekly word count down and post it up somewhere, because it's going to be your goal for this week and the next five weeks.

WHAT IF MY NOVEL IS RUNNING TOO SHORT?

As an acquiring editor, I've declined a lot of novel submissions because they weren't actually novels, but novellas. New writers in particular frequently struggle getting to full novel length.

Many writers' first drafts run a *little* short. That's because the writers are just getting the story down first, and they flesh it out more in the second draft. It's only a problem if it's running *really* short.

If you want to write a full-length novel and you can't figure out how to get to that word count, here are some possible issues.

Your Plot Is More Suited to a Short Story or Novella

It's possible that you just don't have a complex enough story to fill a whole novel. That could be disappointing to realize, but then again, there's nothing wrong with writing a terrific short story or novella. There are plenty of markets for those, too, and you'll learn things as you write the story that you can apply to a full-length novel.

You're Summarizing Too Many Scenes

This is a huge issue with many newer writers. They tell the readers what happened instead of fleshing out the scene.

They might write something like this:

Margaret had promised her sister Alice she'd stop by her house to walk her dog since Alice had to work late that night. When Margaret got there, a black SUV sat in Alice's driveway. Margaret figured it was a friend of Alice's who'd stopped by, but when she looked into the window of the truck, it was empty. She thought it was strange, but went ahead and let herself into Alice's house. Ralph didn't bark or run up to greet her. Alice closed the front door behind her. "Don't move," a man's voice said. She turned back around. A handsome man in a suit pointed a gun at her.

This could be a suspenseful scene, but it's not, because everything's summed up. It ought to read more like this:

Margaret remembered just in time to take the exit to her sister's house. Alice had sent her a desperate text that morning: *I'm going to be at the office till midnight! Can you please, please stop in after work and walk Ralph?* She'd ended the text with three emojis: prayer hands, a smiley face, and a heart.
No problem! Margaret had texted back. She liked walking Ralph, and it had been a while since she'd seen the big, friendly mutt.
As she drove down the tree-lined suburban street, her stomach growled. Fortunately, her sister loved to bake. Maybe there would be leftover muffins or cookies in the kitchen.

Instead of one sentence, we have two paragraphs. We can envision Alice's sedate neighborhood, and we know that Margaret's looking forward to meeting up with an affectionate dog and maybe noshing on something delicious. This is going to make it all the more shocking when Margaret comes face-to-face with a threatening gunman – and all the more worrisome when the dog is nowhere to be found. (By the way, I would never hurt a dog in a story. I'll kill off people, but not dogs.)
If you're doing a lot of summarizing, look for ways to flesh out your scenes. Don't just tell your readers what happened. Let them *experience* it along with the main character.

You're Not Describing Much
One of the most effective ways of evoking an imagined world is through precise description. Doing so as you narrate your story will make a lasting impression on your readers. Readers will be most receptive to learning what people look like, what they're wearing, what they sound like when they talk, how they move, and so on, if you provide these details along with important events.

You Don't Convey the Characters' Thoughts and Feelings

There's a lot going on in your characters' heads and hearts. They imagine saying things they would never actually speak aloud. They wonder about other people's actions, feelings, and motivations. They hope and worry. At different times, they feel confused, elated, and disappointed. For your readers to make a connection with your characters, access their thoughts and feelings.

You're Resolving the Conflict Too Easily

I see writers do this all the time, and I've done it myself more than once. They set up a great conflict…and then they don't make the most of it.

Both brothers want to take over a company…but then, in no time at all, they decide they can run it together.

A woman is falsely accused of stealing…but she easily disproves the accusation.

Three people are stranded on an icy mountain after a small plane crash…but a rescue team comes for them a day later.

When you have a great conflict, don't waste it by resolving it right away. Make it hard for your characters to overcome. Don't be too nice to your characters! The story will be more meaningful if your readers know all that is at stake when characters struggle.

WHAT IF MY NOVEL IS RUNNING TOO LONG?

Some people have this opposite issue. Again, if it's just running a little long, that's not a problem. You can always cut.

If you're on track to write a 150,000-word or even a 250,000-word novel, though, that's an issue. Most agents don't want to represent a novel that long, especially from a debut author.

New writers sometimes think, "Once the agent reads my book, they'll realize it *needs* to be 178,935 words long." The unpleasant truth is, though, that many agents won't read it. They're swamped with submissions, and if they see that word count in your query letter, they'll send a standard rejection letter without even reading your synopsis.

Why? Because it's too hard to sell to publishers. The longer books are, the more they cost to print, and the more publishers have to charge for them. Even more important, it can take a lot of extra marketing dollars to convince readers to plunk down a lot of cash and take on a serious time commitment for an author they don't even know.

Yes, there have been exceptions, but consider that getting published is hard in the first place. Do you want to make it even harder?

This may not be a concern for you if you're self-publishing. Then again, you'll still face the problem of convincing readers to make a big time commitment for an unknown author.

So why *is* your book running so long?

You might be covering too much of your main character's life—his childhood, his boring day at work and school, and so on. People who write memoirs often feel they need to cover every year of their lives in detail, too, instead of focusing on the most interesting parts.

If you've taken on several point of view characters, you may not be able to stay within an average novel length. You may be dragging down the story as you switch from one character to another. Alternately, you may be telling seven or so *different* stories that don't even intersect that much and could be better told from one or two points of view, instead of seven.

I love the painter David Hockney, and he wrote something about this in his book *On Photography*:

"All those attempts to bring everything in around you are part of a naïve belief that you can recreate the whole world. Well, you can't. Where would you put it? Next to the whole world?"

Focus in and find the most interesting material. Stay with it and trust it's enough.

CHECKLIST FOR STEP 15

- [ ] I've figured out my weekly word count goals for this week and the next five weeks.
- [ ] I've hit this week's word count goal.
- [ ] If my novel seems to be running too short or too long, I've considered why that is and I've started to make adjustments.
- [ ] I've backed up my work so far, in case someone steals my computer.

STEP 16: WRITE TO THE MIDPOINT, PART II

In this week or this step, you're going to hit your word count. Simple.

Simple isn't the same as easy, of course. You may find all kinds of things (life, basically) getting in your way. Adapt, don't give up, hang in there, and do the best and the most you can.

You may also be getting in your own way…by procrastinating.

Let's talk about that.

HOW TO STOP PROCRASTINATING

I first learned when I taught at a university that procrastinators are the rule, not the exception. Almost everyone finds it difficult to sit down and write.

Procrastination isn't something to be ashamed of, since it's the norm. *Not* procrastinating is a superpower—a totally attainable one!

Once you figure out how to overcome procrastination, you will have the world on a string. Not only will your writing benefit, but so will your day job, your studies, your relationships, and every part of your life.

Not doing a thing may suck up more time and energy than you realize. And while we might sometimes think of disciplined people as being joyless, research suggests that the exact opposite is true.

Here are a few ways to stop putting off your writing. You may find they apply to other things, too!

Remember That the More You Do It, the Easier It Will Get.
If it feels hard to sit down and work, it may be because it runs counter to the habits you've developed so far. We all have things we do every day, and when we do something else instead, it makes us uncomfortable.

"I don't have enough discipline," we say. But to stop procrastination, it might help to know that if we keep on making ourselves write on a daily or at least somewhat regular basis, after a while, it won't feel uncomfortable. It will be a normal thing to do, like watching TV. The thing that makes it difficult now—habit—is exactly the thing that will make it easy later.

I know many, many writers who are more productive than I am, and I am working on the habit of taking too many internet breaks, but writing is at least something of a habit with me. It no longer feels like an act of great discipline.

Allow Yourself to Do Just a Little Bit.
One of the reasons we procrastinate with many things, particularly with our writing, is that we imagine that we'll need *hours* of uninterrupted time in order to make any progress. It's not true. If you've never been able to establish a regular writing habit, try doing twenty minutes every day. You can even set a timer on your phone, if your phone has that function.

Twenty minutes is nothing. You can't even finish a sitcom in that length of time. But for a creative project, twenty minutes on a regular basis is a big deal. Fair warning, though — you may find yourself getting inspired and going longer.

Give Yourself a Little Reward — Every Time.
This is advice from one of my best friends, and I often forget to follow it! The principle is rock solid, though.

You know how if you're training a dog, you give them a treat every time they do the correct thing? Human behavior gets reinforced in exactly the same way. Reward yourself with a piece of chocolate, a bubble bath, an episode of a TV show you love, a latte, or whatever you think will make the connection in your brain between writing (or any desired habit) and enjoyment.

Here's something you can think about this week if you're writing in anything but omniscient point of view.

HOW TO WRITE IN DEEP POINT OF VIEW

"Deep point of view" is a point of view that allows the reader to be completely immersed in the character's thoughts, feelings, and consciousness. You can achieve deep point of view in either first person or third person.

You can fine-tune point of view in the editing process, but you can also be aware of it in the first draft. Here are two ways to achieve deep point of view.

1. Cut Out "Filtering" Verbs in Third Person Point of View

One of the main ways to do it is to cut or limit verbs such as the following. Many people call them "filtering" verbs because they hold the reader at arm's length from the point of view character.

thought	decided
wondered	believed
knew	noticed
realized	saw
remembered	heard
imagined	felt

Here's an example of how these kinds of verbs might work in a passage that isn't in deep point of view.

> *His eyes felt itchy, and he rubbed them. He wondered if he might be allergic to something on the farm. He thought it seemed likely. He decided he never should've left Seattle.*

If we wanted to deepen the point of view, we might do something like this:

> *He rubbed his itching eyes. Was he allergic to something on the farm? Probably. He never should've left Seattle.*

The second passage is more immediate. Writing in deep point of view also makes it easier to vary your sentence structure. When you use a lot of filtering verbs, it's easy to wind up with sentence after sentence beginning with "I" if you're writing in the first person, and "he" or "she" if you're writing in the third person.

2. Adjust the Voice to the Point of View

When you're writing in first person, getting your main character's voice right makes the point of view deeper. This involves using vocabulary, turns of phrase, and even sentence constructions that fit with the character.

Think about it this way: if you were writing an epic fantasy story from the point of view of an elderly wizard, you probably wouldn't write it in a casual voice with a bunch of contemporary slang. If you were writing from the point of view of a ten-year-old, you probably wouldn't use long, complex, analytical sentences and references to the stock market...unless your protagonist is a truly unusual ten-year-old.

CHECKLIST FOR STEP 16

- [ ] I've hit this week's word count goal.
- [ ] I've considered ways to write in deeper POV.
- [ ] I've backed up my work so far in case my computer gets stolen.

STEP 17: WRITE TO THE MIDPOINT, PART III

IN THIS STEP, ONCE AGAIN, you're going to hit your word count to get to the midpoint. Hopefully, you're making steady progress.

If you're doing a lot of rewriting of what you've already done, however—going back and tweaking sentences, rearranging paragraphs, and so on—then you may be struggling to hit your weekly goals. And I'm going to try to break you of that bad habit right now, because it will get in the way of your success as an author.

HOW TO STOP PERFECTIONISM FROM RUINING YOUR PROGRESS

Constantly rewriting makes you feel like you're a good writer with high standards. When you tell people you haven't finished a draft yet because you're such a perfectionist, you'll get sympathetic nods and murmurs. And as long as it's not finished, you won't have to show it to anyone and risk criticism. By protecting your ego, you're sacrificing your goal: a finished draft.

If you're following this book, rewriting is unnecessary in the steps where you're just hitting your word count. You stopped to revise after you wrote the first three chapters, and you're going to do it again at the midpoint. When you finish a draft, you've got a whole section taking you through the editing process. Polishing up every phrase and sentence now is a waste of time, because in editing, we'll get the story right first and then we polish up the writing style. You're going to throw out whole sentences, paragraphs, and maybe even scenes.

For this reason, being a perfectionist now can actually ruin the editing process later. You won't want to throw away a useless scene if you spent three days making sure it was beautifully written. But if you leave in useless scenes, your whole story will suffer as a result.

A messy first draft is nothing to fear. It doesn't mean you're not a good writer. Successful authors—even the ones you admire the most—write messy first drafts.

Until you've been through it a few times, it's hard to believe how much a draft can improve from the first draft to the final version. Revising and editing is a bigger part of the process than most newer writers realize, but it's best done once you've got the whole story down.

Quit messing around and spending a half hour at a time trying to find the perfect word, or rewriting a long sentence to make two short sentences. For now, just hit your word count.

START SAVING UP IF NECESSARY

In Step 51, to get your book to final draft stage, you're going to get it proofread. You might need to hire a professional proofreader. Proofreading doesn't cost as much as editing, but it isn't cheap.

You may be thinking you can proofread it yourself, and it's true you can eliminate a lot of the mistakes. However, most of us have at least a couple of grammar or spelling issues that we never quite get right. More important, anyone in publishing will tell you it's hard for writers to proofread their own writing because they know what it's *supposed* to say. Their minds go ahead and fill in missing words and glide over mistakes. By the time you get to Step 51, you'll have been staring at this manuscript for a long time, and you'll need a fresh set of eyes.

You may have options other than hiring someone. If you're married to or related to someone who's particularly qualified (someone who has a degree in English, for example), and you can get them to do this for you, that's great! And if you and another writer are both strong proofreaders, you can swap manuscripts.

If you need a sensitivity reader, you may also need to start saving for that. Sensitivity readers charge varying rates for feedback on a full-length novel. Online writers' groups can be one good place to find sensitivity readers.

If you're planning on self-publishing, you'll have other costs as well, including your book cover design, your formatting (unless you learn to do it yourself), your ISBN if you choose to buy one, filing for copyright, and advertising and promotion.

CHECKLIST FOR STEP 17

- [ ] I've hit this week's word count goal.
- [ ] I am resisting the urge to make every sentence perfect in the first draft.
- [ ] I've started saving, if necessary, for proofreading and other anticipated services.
- [ ] I've backed up my work so far in case my computer is hit by a meteor.

STEP 18: WRITE TO THE MIDPOINT, PART IV

You know what your goal is: hit your word count again! And in this chapter, I'm going to talk about an issue that can confound a lot of writers.

UNDERSTANDING PAST TENSE AND PAST PERFECT TENSE

Most novels are written in past tense. Past tense is like this:

Bryn walked to the café.
The dog scratched at the door.

Past perfect tense is a past tense verb plus the past tense of the auxiliary verb "to have." It looks like this:

Bryn had walked to the café.
The dog had scratched at the door.

In a novel that's written in past tense, past perfect tense is used to indicate that the action happens before the time frame of the rest of the action. For instance:

They'd met once before on a cruise ship.
As a child, Arturo had loved the comic books.
The parade had been a tradition in the small town for decades.
She'd expected a very different kind of party.

Why did I make "they had" and "she had" into contractions? In a novel, I always make contractions of "he had," "she had," "I had," "we had," and "they had" for a smoother read. This is a stylistic choice, and it might or might not be your preference.

That's not the real issue I want to discuss, though. Here's where writers run into trouble. They have a long passage that takes place in the past: a week ago, a decade ago, or even centuries ago. They don't want to keep using past perfect tense the whole time, and with good reason: it gets tedious and no fun to read.

How do you solve this problem without being confusing? Easy.

When you begin the long section that's in the past, use the past perfect tense a few times. Break to a new paragraph and continue in simple past tense.

The past perfect tense acts as a signpost to the reader. "Hey, guys, we're going further into the past now. Are you with me? Okay, great."

Here's an example.

The tulips bloomed along the driveway. Crouching down, Sophie yanked a stray weed out of the flowerbed, and then another.

She'd planted them last fall, soon after she'd won the city council election. Her campaign manager had rented out the banquet room at Garazzo's for the victory party.

Sophie's family, friends, and volunteers hugged and ate pizza, their loud conversations punctuated here and there by the pops of champagne corks and accidentally stepped-on balloons.

And we can go on for a page or two in simple past tense at the election party, right up to the time when Sophie meets the man she's dating now.

How do we get out of this flashback? One way is to switch back to past perfect tense for a short paragraph at the end, like this.

By the time the party wound down, Sophie had been talking to Greg for hours. The next day, he'd invited her to dinner, and two months later, he'd proposed.

Another way to get out of the flashback is to simply return the focus to the present day. It could be something like:

Sophie pulled the last weed, straightened up, and headed toward the front door.

Okay, that's it for the lesson in grammar and usage. Have fun writing!

CHECKLIST FOR STEP 18

☐ I've hit this week's word count goal.

☐ I've mastered the use of past perfect tense.

☐ I've backed up all of my work so far to avoid future heartbreak.

STEP 19: WRITE TO THE MIDPOINT, PART V

Well, friends, it's another week of hitting your word count. How are you doing? Hanging in there? Making progress? I hope so!

In this section, I'm going to address some legal questions that writers often ask. The biggest one that I hear all the time is,

CAN I USE SONG LYRICS IN MY NOVEL?

Lots of beginning authors, especially, want to do this. They want to use song lyrics to convey a mood, or sometimes, to create a literal soundtrack for their work—for instance, having the badass character speeding down the road and cranking a certain song, or having the romantic couple slow-dance to a certain song.

Is it okay to put those lyrics in your story? Unless the song is in the public domain, like a lot of traditional Christmas carols or folk songs, you cannot legally put the lyrics in your novel. The songwriter has rights to the work, and so does the publisher. In theory, you can try to get permission, but you'll need to get it from both the songwriter and the publisher. I've worked with licensing songs before in my career, so I know that it's very hard to get permission and it's very expensive.

Hopefully, as a writer, you understand how bad it would feel to have someone else steal your creative work. But no matter how you feel about it, it's copyright infringement. And if you're trying to get published and your story is relying heavily on song lyrics you don't own, it's a huge turnoff for agents and publishers.

But there are three even bigger reasons not to use contemporary song lyrics.

First of all, you may be pushing away everyone in your audience who isn't familiar with the song.

Secondly, they may know the song and hate it. Musical tastes vary quite a bit, and the song could give them a bad impression of your writing.

Thirdly, if a reader doesn't know a song, the lyrics of that song are generally not that impressive. On the page, without the vocals or the music, they can fall flat.

It's up to you as a writer to figure out how to create that emotion that you feel when you hear that song…in your own words. You're a writer. You can do this. If you have your badass character speeding down the road cranking a song, you can mention that he's playing loud music, but you can also write about the ruts in the road under his wheels, the sound of the engine, the thoughts running through his head, the adrenaline pouring through his veins, the way he's gripping the steering wheel…all of that is going to be effective. Your reader is going to feel it.

As I mentioned earlier in the book, you can use song titles, which are not copyrightable. That's why so many books and movies are named after songs. You can name every chapter after a song title if you want, and you can refer to specific songs in the story.

Let's talk about a couple of other common legal questions.

IS IT LEGAL TO USE BRAND NAMES IN MY NOVEL?

In other words, can I refer to Starbucks? Can I refer to a videogame by name? Can I refer to a clothing brand? Can I talk about Twitter?

The answer is yes. It's absolutely okay to talk about your character going to Starbucks or posting on Instagram. I have three cautions here, however.

The first is that you want to make sure most of the things you reference are familiar to most of your readers. The second thing is that pop culture references can make your novel stale and dated very fast. For that reason, I recommend using pop culture references in particular very sparingly. Finally, you can't make up lies about companies and brands, because that could lead to legal trouble.

CAN I WRITE A NOVEL ABOUT SOMEONE ELSE'S FICTIONAL CHARACTERS?

If the characters are from a work that's in the public domain, then yes. That's how *Romeo and Juliet* became *West Side Story*, and the novel *Emma* became the 1995 movie *Clueless*.

If the characters are from a work that's not in the public domain, then no, you can't write and publish stories about them.

That being said, we have a strong tradition of fanfiction in this contemporary era. Many people write fanfic and put it on certain websites. A lot of authors and copyright holders don't mind fanfic because the writer isn't making money off of it. However, a few authors abhor fanfic and condemn it on their websites. I suggest finding out what an author's disposition is to fanfic before writing it.

CHECKLIST FOR STEP 19

- [ ] I've hit this week's word count goal.
- [ ] I've made sure that my novel doesn't include copyright infringement.
- [ ] I've backed up my work so that if my computer crashes, I won't be emotionally destroyed.

STEP 20: HIT THE MIDPOINT

When you hit your word count this week, you'll be more or less halfway done with your first draft.

But you may be starting to have misgivings about your story. If you aren't, that's fantastic, and you shouldn't! But if you are, that's also normal.

You may have thought of one or even three or four shiny new ideas that all sound better, and more "you." You may even be tempted to scrap the story and start again.

WHAT SHOULD I DO WHEN YOU'RE NOT FEELING YOUR NOVEL?

You should probably finish it anyway.

It's actually fine to toggle between a few projects. It's okay to set something aside to marinate, begin a new thing, and come back to your first thing.

But if you've never finished anything? Then especially, you should finish. You can study and read up and write all you want, but there are things that you can *only* learn by finishing a story. Besides, you need to know you're capable of doing it.

Some first drafts feel excruciating: soulless, cheesy, clichéd, or all of the above. Maybe you think there are a thousand stories like it. Maybe you realize there are *no* stories like it, and you wonder if it will have a tiny audience. You might tell yourself: *This story is awful. Why did I even start it?*

As you plug away, you'll think of new ideas and encounter new insights into the characters. It *will* get better as you go along.

The One Question That Can Keep Your Writing on Track

If you *are* starting to doubt your story, ask yourself this:

Why do I want to write THIS story?

Out of all the stories in the world you could have picked, you chose this one. There's a personal reason why you picked this story, even if you're not aware of it yet.

I once heard someone from Pixar talk about this principle. The excellent movie *Up* began with the drawing of a house being carried away by hundreds of balloons. The artist who drew it had a lot of responsibilities and pressures, like most of us do, and the drawing symbolized his longing to float away from it all and go far, far away. Preserving that fantasy of escapism was crucial to the movie.

I believe we all start writing projects with an emotional need or something we're yearning to say, even if we aren't aware of exactly what it is. Identifying it can make it easier to figure out what we're doing and give us confidence.

Anyway, nobody wants to buy your unfinished book. Editors don't want it. Agents don't want to represent it unless you are already at least a bit famous. Readers don't want to read it. So finish what you started.

If you're halfway through your story, that's huge. Way to go!

CHECKLIST FOR STEP 20

- [ ] I've now written about half of my first draft!
- [ ] I've addressed any misgivings I've had about my novel.
- [ ] I've backed up my work so far in case an elephant stomps on and crushes my computer.

STEP 21: READ THROUGH THE FIRST HALF

Settle in. It's time to read what you've written so far! But first, let me give you a few examples of things you *shouldn't* worry about:

- badly written sentences
- unnatural dialogue
- overused words
- clichéd metaphors

You might notice some bad habits in your writing, like putting a semicolon in every other sentence or using an adverb after every "said" in sight (*she said grimly, he said hopefully,* and so on). If you do, you can take care to avoid doing that as you write the second half of your book. You don't need to fix style problems in the writing you've already done. Worry about it later.

However, you should look for one or two big issues and make some notes about them on your Fix List. Here are a few things you might ask yourself.

Are there any plot holes?
A plot hole is a failure in story logic.

It may be a plot point that contradicts something else in the story.

It might involve someone being able to do something they weren't able to do before—or *not* being able to do something we'd expect him to be able to do.

It might simply fly in the face of rational thinking (e.g., the type of thing that makes a reader ask, "Why didn't she simply do this instead?")

If you realize there's a plot hole in your story, you may feel despondent. Don't! In my experience, they're almost always fixable, even if the solution doesn't spring to mind immediately. Give it a few days. You'll figure it out!

Are any of the characters two-dimensional, inconsistent, or unlikeable? To be clear, not all characters are intended to be likeable. But if you want the readers to root for your main characters, now is a good time to make sure you're setting them up that way.

Naturally, your main characters can be quirky or flawed. But if your character's flaw is that he's too aggressive and he'll learn better over the course of the story, you still can't have him kick a puppy in Chapter One. Everyone will hate him. *I'll* hate him.

If you want readers to like your hero and he's snarky, that's probably fine, but if he makes fun of someone for being ugly or poor, your readers aren't going to laugh. They'll think your hero is a jerk, and before you know it, you'll be the proud owner of multiple one-star reviews. (Pro tip: snark works best when directed toward mean people with power.)

"Two-dimensional characters" are characters who don't feel like real people. Villains often fall into this category, especially in a first draft: they go around being evil because they like to be evil. A two-dimensional character may be a walking stereotype of a rich trophy wife or a small-town yokel.

You need to find the humanity in characters like these. Maybe the rich trophy wife *is* vain and materialistic, but also has a sharp sense of humor. Maybe the small-town yokel *is* backwards and slow on the uptake, but he's also kind and checks in on his grandmother every Sunday. If they're minor characters, it doesn't take much to round them out.

If any of your characters are inconsistent in their words or actions, it'll frustrate your readers, and that goes double for your main characters. That's not to say your characters can't take rash or surprising actions. It's exciting when they do! But we need to understand their reasons for doing it, and those reasons need to be consistent with everything else we know about them.

Make some notes about two or three high-level things you want to fix before moving on. And even though you're reading your work so far with a critical eye, I hope you appreciate how far you've come!

CHECKLIST FOR STEP 21

☐ I've read through my draft so far.

☐ I've noted one or two important things I want to fix.

☐ I've backed up my work so far, because I'm smart like that.

STEP 22: EVALUATE YOUR PACING

In the last step, you may or may not have made notes about the pacing of your story. Pacing can be a tricky thing to address, but it's so important for the reader's enjoyment.

"Pacing" refers to the speed at which the story progresses. If the story is too slow, readers get bored. If it's too fast, it feels rushed. When this is the case, readers don't care as much about the story, because they didn't even have enough time to get to know the characters or understand what's at stake.

Ask yourself if it seems too slow or too rushed overall. You also want the pace to be consistent. You don't want some sections of the book to move slowly while others feel rushed.

HOW TO EVALUATE THE CONSISTENCY OF YOUR PACING

To see if the pace is consistent, make a list of the big, important events that have happened in your book. At the midpoint, you'll likely have two or three of them.

For instance, if I were writing a pirate novel, I might have a list that looked something like this.

Tom joins the crew of a whaling ship
pirates capture ship; Tom hides in the hold, living off hard tack
one pirate, Horace, finds Tom two weeks later, but chooses not to turn him in

These are the big turning points. They may not even be my personal favorite scenes, but they are the scenes in which everything changes.

Once you've got these important turning points, write down the page number where each scene begins. It might look something like this:

Tom joins the crew of a whaling ship – p. 1

pirates capture ship; Tom hides in the hold, living off hard tack – p. 119

one pirate, Horace, finds Tom two weeks later, but chooses not to turn him in – p. 131

These events don't have to be at perfectly regular intervals. It may be that big events in the last third or so of the novel are closer together, building up to a satisfying finale.

In my example, I may have a huge gap between event #1 and event #2. Then event #3 happens pretty fast in the story, even though weeks go by between event #2 and event #3. After evaluating, I can see I need to even out my pacing.

IF YOU CAN'T TELL, ASK

Beta readers can be helpful in evaluating your overall pacing. They may be particularly helpful when you give them just *one thing* to give you feedback on– and because you're only asking about the one thing, they may be more willing to do it, too.

Reach out to them and say something like, "Hey, I wonder if you could read through what I've got on my novel so far and tell me if it feels too slow or too rushed. I'd need it back in a week, but that's the only thing I need to know."

Sometimes, just *thinking* about asking a specific question like that can open our eyes to the answer. If you asked a professional editor about your pacing, what do you think she'd say?

WRITE UP YOUR EVALUATION

Write one or two sentences down about your pacing. It should look something like:

- *My whole novel so far is too rushed.*

- *My whole novel so far is too slow.*
- *My novel so far has inconsistent pacing because the two most exciting things happen too close together.*
- *My novel so far has decent pacing, but the two scenes with my main character and her mother drag, and they may not even be necessary to the story.*

You get the idea. Write the problem down, because that makes it easier to fix it.

And how will you do that? We'll talk about that in the next step!

CHECKLIST FOR STEP 22

☐ I've evaluated the pacing in my story so far.

☐ I've asked others for help with my pacing if necessary.

☐ I've backed up my work so far.

STEP 23: FIX YOUR PACING

It's a lot easier to address your pacing now than it is to wrestle with the pacing in an entire finished draft. If by some miracle, you've found that you don't have any pacing problems, you can use this time to work on one of the other high-level issues you identified with the draft so far.

HOW TO FIX A STORY THAT'S TOO SLOW

If your story is dragging, look for the following opportunities to make it better.

Does it have an unnecessary prologue? Or even an unnecessary Chapter One?

Does the prologue or Chapter One pile on information about the backstory? (This is usually referred to as an "info dump.")

Are there passages—or even whole scenes, or whole chapters—that don't contribute much to the plot?

Does the dialogue include a lot of small talk about things that don't matter?

Once you've considered the issue, you can probably find some ways to tighten up your story and keep it moving along.

HOW TO FIX A STORY THAT'S TOO RUSHED

For this issue, go back to Step 15 and look at the ways to address a manuscript that's running too short.

Also, look for places where a character's decisions, actions, or abilities seem to come out of nowhere. If it's a romance, does he fall desperately in love with someone he's met twice? Then you're going to have to go back and add one or two scenes where these two interact and connect. If it's a fantasy, does she go from simple farm girl to skilled warrior in thirty pages? You're going to have to go back and flesh out that training scene…and maybe show her barely survive one skirmish, and then train some more.

HOW TO FIX INCONSISTENT PACING

Here, you may be adding or deleting scenes to make sure that the big, exciting moments happen at more or less regular intervals. In the process, you'll probably figure out how to focus on the most important and interesting parts.

You may not even have to add or cut whole scenes, though. You might realize that one scene went into unnecessary detail, while a couple of other scenes are skeletal and need to be fleshed out.

Editing for pacing may seem daunting at first, especially if you've gotten used to the story as it is, but just diving into it is half the challenge.

CHECKLIST FOR STEP 23

- [ ] I've improved the pacing in my story so far.
- [ ] I've backed up my work so far, because I don't want to lose all these improvements.

STEP 24: FIX THOSE ONE OR TWO THINGS

You've read over your WIP so far and you've made some notes about things that need to be worked on. You've also improved the pacing.

This week, dig in and fix the one or two issues you identified with your draft so far. It could be a shaky plot point, a troublesome character, or one particular scene that isn't working. Focus on those elements and don't worry about anything else. Improving them will give you renewed energy for writing the rest of your story.

MORE WRITER MATH

You also need to figure out your word count targets for the next ten weeks (or the next ten steps) to complete your first draft.

Start with your desired word count. It's okay if you've adjusted this a little, but try to keep it in the typical range for your genre.

Subtract the word count you have so far.

Divide the remainder by ten.

For example, it might look like this:

90,0000 (desired length for my science fiction novel)
39, 888 - (words I've written so far)
50,112 (words I still need to write)

50,112 / 10 = 5011 words a week

It's okay if you didn't get quite to half your desired word count. The second half usually flows more quickly than the first, especially when you've already stopped a couple of times to do some editing. You've already worked out some of the kinks and issues that were irritating your subconscious creative brain and slowing you down.

Is your novel going to come in at your exact targeted word count? Well, no, probably not. But your weekly word count will keep you on track and keep a rough idea in your head about the proportions of the finished draft.

CHECKLIST FOR STEP 24

- [ ] I've fixed the one or two major issues in my draft so far.
- [ ] I've backed up my work so far in case a power surge fries my computer.
- [ ] I've figured out my weekly word count targets for the next ten weeks.

STEP 25: WRITE TO THE END, PART I

It's time to write the second half of your novel! You might want to reassess your schedule and figure out other ways to make time for writing. If you made a playlist at the beginning, you might want to use it again…or you might want to make a new one now. You might even want to treat yourself to a scented candle that you light only when you're writing.

Speaking of sounds and scents, here's something to think about this week.

HOW TO USE ALL FIVE SENSES IN YOUR WRITING

When we talk about description in writing, we're usually talking about *visual* description. But many of us as writers tend to neglect the other senses: hearing, taste, smell, and touch. By layering in more of these non-visual details, we can help readers get even more lost in the story—almost as though it's happening to them in real life.

Cue the Soundtrack
One of my friends likes to watch horror movies with her husband and son. When a movie gets too scary, though, one of them covers his ears.

That's right—his ears, not his eyes. Why? Because he still wants to see what happens, and he's learned that it's much less frightening without the sound. The creaking of a slowly opening door, a little girl's disembodied voice, a loud heartbeat, and so many other sounds can heighten the emotional effect.

We can add sound effects to increase the emotional impact of scenes: a purring cat, a crackling fire, the click of high heels on a hard floor, or a crash of thunder.

We can also layer in other sounds to set a mood and help the reader escape into the story. In a cave, we might note the sounds of dripping water and the echoing of our steps and our voices. In downtown Los Angeles, we might describe the sounds of the traffic and the whirring of a police helicopter above.

Tell Them How It Feels

The sensation of touch helps the reader merge with the character. Describe the cold wind against the character's face, making her eyes water—the tears freezing on her cheeks. Write about the hard, frozen ground under her boots, and her feet going numb inside them. Suddenly, the reader isn't just thinking about a January trek, but experiencing it.

Even when your characters are sitting around talking, you can write about the feel of a velvet upholstery under someone's hand, or the warmth of the mug of coffee.

Hijack Your Reader's Emotions With Scent

Smell is probably the most underutilized sense in writing, which is too bad, because the impact can be immediate and visceral. We have gut-level reactions to smells. They bypass our logic and go right to the most primitive parts of our brains. Smells also evoke memories in a direct way that no other sensations can.

A disgusting smell can underscore an alarming or dire scene. A good smell can elevate a happy moment in the story. Romance authors are always having lovers notice one another's particular, appealing scents, and why not? Even though we think of ourselves as rational beings, scent is still a factor in our attraction to others.

Add Some Flavor

Even a mention of the taste of food will keep your readers' attention, even if it makes them hungry. (One of my proofreaders pointed out that a character might also taste blood after getting punched in the mouth. Good point!)

CHECKLIST FOR STEP 25

- [ ] I've hit my word count.
- [ ] I've made conscious attempts to appeal to the senses of sound, touch, smell, or taste.
- [ ] I've backed up my work so far, lest it disappear like the moon on a cloudy night.

STEP 26: WRITE TO THE END, PART II

In this section, I'm going to cover a question you may have had at some point.

WHAT'S WRONG WITH ADVERBS?

The author Stephen King famously said, "I believe the road to hell is paved with adverbs." He was hardly the first to come to that conclusion; most editors in publishing houses, like me, also enjoy plucking them out of manuscripts. I'll talk about why, but first I'll make sure that we all remember what an adverb is.

An adverb usually modifies a verb—or, to think about it another way, an adverb supplies extra information or commentary on a verb. Occasionally, an adverb modifies another adverb, which modifies a verb. In the sentence, "He stepped very quietly into the room," *very* is an adverb modifying *quietly*, which modifies *stepped*.

Most adverbs end in the suffix -ly, but some adverbs, such as "very," don't. Many words that end in -ly are *not* adverbs, because English is ridiculous.

Here's why most editors and authors avoid excessive use of adverbs.

An Adverb + Verb Can Often Be Replaced By a More Vivid Verb
Here are a few sentences with adverbs and how they can be rewritten with a more vivid verb.

Before: "He moved quickly to the window."
After: "He rushed to the window."
Before: "She gracefully entered the room."
After: "She glided into the room."

When you omit most of the adverbs, you have more variety in the verbs you use throughout the story, and the overall effect is stronger.

An Adverb Often Supplies Unnecessary Commentary
Every Monday, my husband and I watch a movie together. When I watch a movie at home, I have a terrible habit of commenting on the obvious. "He doesn't trust her yet." "Oooh, she's not going to like that!"

Because my husband is patient, he doesn't get annoyed. However, most people dislike obvious commentary. In a manuscript, adverbs are often a lot like me as a home movie viewer, telling you things that are obvious.

"Unexpectedly, a ferret fell from the light fixture."

Unless ferrets have been falling willy-nilly, you don't have to tell me that this is unexpected.

"I'm going to kill you!" he yelled angrily.

Yeah, I gathered he was angry.

Most Contemporary Readers Prefer Straightforward Prose
Did you notice that when you replace the adverb, the sentence is usually shorter?

If you read 19th-century novels, you'll find longer passages of description, longer lines of dialogue, and a lot of longer sentences in general. You're also likely to find more adverbs! Back then, books weren't competing with radio, TV, and movies…mediums that often move quickly. Contemporary readers are used to a somewhat faster pace, which is one reason why adverbs are much less popular now than they used to be.

Even back in the 19th century, Nathaniel Hawthorne had it right when he said, "Easy reading is damn hard writing." Clear, direct writing only looks easy, and when you revise, you may make many changes to clarify your sentences and keep readers from stumbling over passages.

Is It Ever Okay to Use Adverbs?
Of course. Although English *is* ridiculous, adverbs wouldn't exist if they weren't useful. Now and again, you're going to run into a situation where the sentence actually does sound better if you keep the adverb. Trust your ear. Listen to your editors…but if you have an editor who thinks you should *never* use an adverb, they're taking a solid principle way too far.

CHECKLIST FOR STEP 26

- [ ] I've hit my word count.
- [ ] I've avoided unnecessary adverbs.
- [ ] I've backed up my work.

STEP 27: WRITE TO THE END, PART III

As you try to hit your word count every week, you may be struggling to fit it in with the rest of your schedule. If you haven't been doing it already, you might want to give writing sprints a try.

HOW TO USE WRITING SPRINTS

A writing sprint is a way to focus on nothing but writing for a short amount of time. There are two ways to do them.

1. Set a timer for a half hour. In that time, get as much writing on your project as you can, as fast as you can.

You might be surprised at how much you can get done in that short window of time!

2. Set a word count goal, such as 500 or 1000 words. Start writing, and don't do anything else until you reach that goal.

With either of these approaches, you're training your brain to focus. You're realizing, more and more, that you don't need a big chunk of time to make progress on your novel. You're eliminating distractions. Which leads me to the next point...

INTERNET BLOCKERS

By now, you know a lot about your own writing process. One of the things you may have noticed is a habit to toggle back and forth between your work and the distractions of the internet. For instance, you might browse a favorite social media platform for a few minutes whenever you get stuck.

If you do this, I have bad news for you: your favorite social media platform doesn't hold the answer to your creative problem, and because you have to re-focus when you turn back to your manuscript again, this habit can grind your progress to a crawl. Don't feel bad, though! This is extremely common.

I recommend the use of internet blockers. Many of these apps will allow you to block the websites where you waste the most time, for whatever time period you choose. (You probably *don't* want to block the whole internet, in case you need to look something up.)

I'm not going to recommend one in particular, but please do your research and make sure it's a reputable one before you install it. You don't want to be downloading a bunch of malware by mistake.

If you use an internet blocker, you might be surprised by how often you automatically toggle over to your favorite sites…almost without even thinking about it. Cutting these addictive sites out of your writing process may give you a big productivity boost.

CHECKLIST FOR STEP 27

- [ ] I've hit my word count.
- [ ] I've used word sprints and/or I've tried an internet blocker if I'm having trouble focusing.
- [ ] I've backed up my work.

STEP 28: WRITE TO THE END, PART IV

YOU'RE GETTING CLOSE TO FINISHING your first draft. That should be exciting, right?

But sometimes this is exactly when a part of our brains starts to panic. After all, talking about creating isn't risky. Finishing a creative project is.

ARE THE DEMONS TRYING TO LURK BACK IN?

You may find yourself suddenly plagued by your old demons of fear and self-doubt. Fear that your work won't be any good. Doubt that you'll be able to make a first draft into a final draft you can proudly share with the world.

And because these demons are super sneaky, they may not even sound like fear and self-doubt. They may show up disguised as perfectly rational arguments for giving up on your novel.

"Let's be realistic," these demons say. "Let's be reasonable." And oh-so-reasonably, they try to convince you to throw your dreams in the trash. Don't fall for it.

Here are a couple of arguments your fear and self-doubt might make.

This wasn't actually a good time to write a novel, because of (insert new development in life here.)

Don't get me wrong: if you're dealing with a truly dire situation, you may need to set your project aside for a while. But people often set aside their novel writing for reasons that aren't dire at all. They decide the timing isn't right because they're planning their parents' fiftieth anniversary party. Or because they started a new job. They think, "I'll wait until life settles down."

I'll let you in on a secret: life rarely settles down. It's usually bumpy. It's usually complicated.

Most successful authors didn't start out independently wealthy, with trouble-free lives. They didn't write their first novel while sitting in their large, quiet home in the mountains overlooking a lake. For the most part, they wrote their first (and often their second, third, and fourth) novels in the midst of stress and chaos. They wrote them in the morning before they left for their jobs, or after they managed to feed their kids and get them in bed.

If you're going to write a book, you're going to have to do it in the middle of everything else going on in your messy life, because if you're like most of us, you're not going to get any other options.

You can make another excuse to quit once again…or this time can be different. This time, in spite of everything, you can get it done.

But here's another thing your demons might be saying.

If I were going to be a writer, I would've done it by now. I've missed my window.
This kind of thinking is pure garbage. Set it aside right now.

Too many of us talk ourselves out of new ventures and adventures in later decades of life. And I've heard people *under thirty* wonder if they've missed their chance to be a writer. That's bananas!

Raymond Chandler, the master of detective fiction, began writing when he was forty-four years old. Bram Stoker wrote *Dracula* at the age of fifty. Anna Sewell was in her mid-fifties when she penned *Black Beauty*. At sixty-six, Frank McCourt published his memoir *Angela's Ashes*. It won the Pulitzer Prize. Harriet Doerr published her debut novel *Stones for Ibarra* at the age of seventy-four. It won a National Book Award.

Older writers have a huge advantage: they have more lived experience. And what's more inspiring than someone embracing their creative passion in their fifties, their seventies, or their nineties?

You haven't missed your window. There is no window. It's a wide-open space.

If you want to write a novel, then now is the perfect time to write a novel.

CHECKLIST FOR STEP 28

- [ ] I've hit my word count.
- [ ] I've brushed aside most of my fears and doubts.
- [ ] I still have a healthy fear of losing my novel, though, so I've backed up my work so far.

STEP 29: WRITE TO THE END, PART V

IN THIS SECTION, I'M GOING to talk to you about commas. They seem like such a tiny issue, but even professional editors occasionally disagree about usage. One thing almost all editors agree on, though, is that comma splices need to be fixed. When I'm reading manuscripts from newer writers, they frequently contain comma splices.

HOW TO RECOGNIZE AND AVOID COMMA SPLICES

A comma splice is an instance of joining two complete sentences with a mere comma. Here are a few examples.

"Jamal shoved a bookcase in front of the door, Kendra turned off the lights."

"I ordered a slice of peach pie, the server brought me chocolate cake."

"She didn't want to attend the ball, her feet still hurt from the last one."

On either side of the comma, there's a complete sentence. How can you tell? Because there's a subject and a verb, and it makes sense if it stands alone. If you have two main clauses that stand on their own as complete sentences, a mere comma isn't enough to hold them together—properly, anyway.

Luckily, there are a few easy ways to fix comma splices.

Use a period and break it up into two sentences.
"Jamal shoved a bookcase in front of the door. Kendra turned off the lights."

"I ordered a slice of peach pie. The server brought me chocolate cake."

Use a conjuction.
"Jamal shoved a bookcase in front of the door and Kendra turned off the lights."

"I ordered a slice of peach pie, but the server brought me chocolate cake."

Use a semicolon if the second sentence continues or builds on the thought.
Semicolons are fairly out of style in some quarters, and any good fiction editor will slap your hand if you overuse them, but I like them in moderation. They work best when the second part continues the thought.

"She didn't want to attend the ball; her feet still hurt from the last one."

Once in a while, a comma splice might feel like the best choice in terms of style. If you feel there's a *compelling reason* to break the rules, go ahead and do it. Just be aware that to some literary agents and editors, it still might look like a mistake.

CHECKLIST FOR STEP 29

- [ ] I've hit my word count.
- [ ] I've started avoiding comma splices.
- [ ] I've backed up my work in order to avoid a tragedy.

STEP 30: WRITE TO THE END, PART VI

SELF-CARE FOR WRITERS

As you close in on finishing your book, I hope you'll practice self-care and stay healthy.

Many people think of writing as an easy job. Stare out the window. Sip your coffee. Type out a fabulous scene. And there's some truth to that! Writing can be a true pleasure. I'd never do it if that weren't the case. But there are some health issues associated with writing.

Here are some health hazards people deal with when they spend a lot of time writing.

The problem: lack of sleep.
Writers who work full-time, and/or are parents or caregivers, often skimp on sleep to get their writing done, staying up late or dragging themselves up out of bed before dawn.

Many of us are perversely proud of ourselves for functioning on little sleep. I am guilty of this myself!

That's probably because we don't hear enough about the necessity of sleep to good health. When we're sleep-deprived, we're less sharp mentally. Our bodies produce too much cortisol, a hormone that can slow metabolism, raise blood pressure, and make us more susceptible to infections, depression, and mental illness. In my own experience, when I start noticing signs of depression, getting good sleep is an effective defense.

The solution: get some rest, obviously.
It's not worth hitting any self-imposed deadline if you make yourself sick or depressed in the process. You are more important than any story. Take care of yourself, and you'll be more productive in the long run. Even more important, you'll be happier.

The problem: stress and anxiety.
For writers, an ordinary day may include a bloody battle scene, the death of a beloved figure, or a bitter breakup. Conflict is vital to a good story. It's all in our heads, but our brains aren't actually that great at separating fiction from real life. When we write about strife, sorrow, or trauma, we often have some of the same physiological responses as we would have in real life, and that can take a toll.

There are real-life pressures involved with writing, too, as there are with any job. Deadlines, difficulties with projects, and rejections all add to a person's stress.

The solution: walk it off.
Even a short walk will help you release writing stress. And if you're feeling that stress because you're creatively stuck, there's no better way to get unstuck.

The problem: repetitive motion injuries.
Hunching over a keyboard for hours can lead to tight neck and shoulder muscles and even pinched nerves. I've experienced the latter personally, after a period of working long hours, including a few all-nighters. It's no joke—it's very painful, and you can't do *any* work until it gets better.

Writers are also susceptible to tendonitis in their hands. This can lead to carpal tunnel syndrome, a nerve condition that can become serious and require surgery.

The solution: stretch at regular intervals throughout the day.
You might want to set alarms on your computer or phone. You can find easy stretches for computer users on medical websites.

The problem: general neglect.
Finally, writing can simply distract us from caring about our health. When we're caught up in the world and the events of a story – and especially when we have a deadline to hit – we may not care much about basic things.

The solutions:
1. *Drink water.*
If you drink coffee, soda, or alcohol while you're working, replace some of those servings with H20. It helps you think more clearly, and it's good for your digestion, your skin, and the health of your kidneys.

2. *Eat some fruits and vegetables.*
Hey, nobody likes a writer with scurvy! Just kidding. If you get scurvy, people will still love you, but you don't want to deal with it. Eat some fruits and vegetables so you get enough vitamin C, beta carotene, and other important nutrients.

3. *Try some yoga.*
Morning or evening yoga is also a great way to stretch, and it calms your mind at the same time.

Every time you do something to take care of your physical well-being, it's good for your mental health, too, because you're sending yourself a message that you're important. And you are!

CHECKLIST FOR STEP 30

- [ ] I've hit my word count.
- [ ] I'm making a conscious effort to take care of myself.
- [ ] I've backed up my work so that it won't suddenly and mysteriously disappear from this earth without a trace.

STEP 31: WRITE TO THE END, PART VII

This week as you hit your word count, I'm going to share some advice on writing fight scenes. You've probably got one in there somewhere if you're writing an action adventure novel, a thriller, or a fantasy novel, and a fight scene can be a part of a novel of any genre.

I'm a peace-loving person in real life, but I love writing fight scenes, and I include them in my paranormal romance novels. If you've got one in your story, here are some things to consider!

4 TIPS FOR WRITING FIGHT SCENES

1. Don't give us the blow by blow...literally.
If you're writing a swordfight or a boxing match, you don't want to detail every single thrust or every single punch. That's going to be mind-numbingly boring. You'll want to do some consolidating and highlighting the most important moments.

2. Don't overdo dialogue and internal monologue.
There's a tradition in literature and film of people bantering as they have a swordfight: think *Three Musketeers, Star Wars,* or *The Princess Bride*. It's a tad unrealistic, but it's also fun. In my opinion, it works better in fantasy and science fiction than stories that take place in the real world.

In general, if it's nonstop action and your characters are fighting for their lives, they're going to be out of breath and focused on the battle. Under those conditions, dialogue is going to be short and to the point.

Their thoughts are also going to focus on the fight. Your character isn't likely to notice that a bystander is wearing fancy shoes or think about what they're going to have for dinner that night. They're focused on survival.

3. Make us feel it.
If your character is in fight mode, they're not only going to be breathing hard, but their heart will likely be pounding, and they're probably going to have adrenaline crashing through their body. If they take a punch or a stab, make us feel that, too, keeping in mind that the adrenaline may make it hurt less until after the fight is over.

When you give readers those physiological responses, they start feeling them too, and the scene feels a lot more gripping and exciting.

4. Consider shorter sentences and shorter paragraphs.
Making many of those sentences shorter and those paragraphs tighter can mirror the focused mentality of your character. It increases the impact and the drama.

Don't have any fight scenes? You can still take some advice from this chapter. If your character is scared, let's get those physiological reactions: the pulse slamming in the neck, the knees shaking. If it's a shocking, dramatic scene, consider shortening the sentences and paragraphs for impact.

CHECKLIST FOR STEP 31

- [ ] I've hit my word count.
- [ ] If I'm writing a fight scene or a very dramatic scene, I've taken advice from this chapter; otherwise, I've filed it away for future use.
- [ ] I've backed up my work so far because I have a modicum of common sense.

STEP 32: WRITE TO THE END, PART VIII

In this chapter, we're going to talk about...

AVOIDING PASSIVE VOICE

Writing in active voice makes your writing more interesting to read. A lot of passive voice makes it sound boring, and often it's less clear. But what is passive voice?

Passive voice is when the subject of the sentence is acted upon by the verb instead of doing the verb. Here are a couple of examples of passive voice, and I'll fix them to make them active.

"In the battle, mistakes were made."

That's passive voice because the subject is "mistakes," and the verb "made" is done to the subject. To fix that, I'm going to talk about who actually makes the mistakes.

"The general made mistakes in the battle."

This is in active voice, because the general is doing something. (By the way, in politics, the corporate world, and in public relations statements, you'll often see people use passive voice as a way to shift, evade, or minimize responsibility or blame.)

Here's another example of a sentence in passive voice.

"A Christmas carol was sung."

To change that, we could say something like,

"The crowd sang a Christmas carol."

Two Things You Need to Know About the Passive Voice

1. It's fine to use it once in a while.
There may be times when you're writing a novel that a sentence in passive voice sounds better and works better in a paragraph than active voice. It's okay if used sparingly.

2. The word "was" (or "is," if you're writing in present tense) doesn't automatically mean the sentence is in passive voice.
Let me explain. If I write:
"Tasha was a lawyer."
That's not passive voice. Nothing is being done to the subject of the sentence. "Was" here is a state of being.
Is it okay to use the verb "was"? Absolutely. If you try to write a past tense story without the words "was" and "were," it's going to sound weird.
However, "was" *can* be a weak verb, so when you use it, you want to look at that sentence and make sure there isn't a stronger verb you can use and a more vivid way to write it. For instance:
"I was terrified."
Mmm, we can do better than that. How about:
"My heart hammered in my chest."
That's better! (By the way, I have lists of ways to describe emotions on my blog, so check out bryndonovan.com if you want to.)
Let's say we have this sentence:
"Chen was tired of waiting."
Instead of that, we might say:
"Chen sighed and looked at his watch for the third time."
That's a more interesting way to write about Chen's impatience. Let's do one more.
"The cottage was charming."
What does that even mean? Let's provide some details instead.
"Flowers bloomed in the window boxes of the bright yellow cottage."
Okay, that does sound charming.
To conclude: sentences with "was" or "were" can sometimes be instances of passive voice. They can sometimes be places where you could be doing more showing and less telling. And sometimes, a sentence with "was" in it is just fine.

CHECKLIST FOR STEP 32

- [ ] I've hit my word count.
- [ ] I've avoided passive voice this week except when I truly believe it's the best choice.
- [ ] I've avoided the word "was" this week in cases where there are more interesting and clear ways to convey the idea.
- [ ] I've backed up my work.

STEP 33: WRITE TO THE END, PART IX

How are you going to stay motivated to hit your word count during this step? Motivation is an ongoing issue as you finish a draft, which is why I address it several times in this book. One thing that can keep you going as you finish your draft—and go through the possibly intense process of revising it—is saying positive affirmations.

AFFIRMATIONS FOR WRITERS

I've shared affirmations through my newsletter before, and while many people email back to tell me they like them, at least one person always emails me back to tell me affirmations are stupid. I keep sharing them anyway. Like any sensible writer, I accept the fact that I'm not for everyone.

Some people see affirmations as New Age foolishness. All I care about is that they work.

Repetition is key. When you say something out loud, on many different occasions, that thought becomes easily accessible in your brain. This isn't New Age talk at all, but basic brain science: the thoughts you have most often are the easiest to access. What's easier to remember—your password to a website you log onto regularly or a password to a website you haven't visited in five years? The first one, of course. You use it frequently, so it's top of mind.

We start to believe things we hear over and over. All of us know this instinctively. Think of a morally repugnant statement: something evil that goes against your most basic values. What if someone dared you to say it out loud, every morning, for a month? You wouldn't want to do it, because you'd be afraid you'd start to believe it.

If you've had the experience of being told something negative about yourself over and over as a child, either by adults or other children ("You'll never amount to anything!" "You're weird." "You're ugly!"), then you know how easy it is to internalize messages. The good news is that you can internalize positive messages, too.

When you first use a positive affirmation, your brain will argue against it. With repetition, this resistance will become weaker. You'll begin to be persuaded, and the affirmation will crowd out more negative thoughts.

Settle on a few, or several, affirmations about your writing and say them out loud every morning. Saying them out loud engages more parts of your brain, so it's more powerful than thinking or reading them.

Here are a bunch of sample affirmations about writing. Choose some you like, or come up with your own. (And while you're at it, you can write affirmations about every part of your life: your friends and family, your health and appearance, your marriage, your finances, or your mental state. They can change your life.)

I write quickly and effortlessly.

I find time to write every day.

I have enough energy to do my day job and still write.

I am staggeringly prolific.

I am abundantly talented.

I can always think of what to write next.

I have interesting ideas and a fresh perspective.

Music, books, and interesting conversations keep me inspired as a writer.

I am a master storyteller.

Every time I write, I get a little better at it.

There are readers out there who love the kind of story I'm working on now.

I love writing.

You might write some affirmations that directly contradict your negative self-talk. Look back at Step 1, in the *Make Room* section, for more inspiration on this.

CHECKLIST FOR STEP 33

- [ ] I've hit my word count.
- [ ] (optional) I've tried out a few writing affirmations.
- [ ] I've backed up my work so far, because if I lost it, no amount of affirmations would be able to cheer me up.

STEP 34: WRITE TO THE END, PART X

How's everything going? Hopefully, your novel is progressing, and if it's stalled out a time or two, no worries. You're only human, and all writers encounter dry spells, roadblocks, and flat-out emergencies. Be good to yourself and keep moving forward.

Since you're almost done with your first draft, let's talk about a question that confounds many emerging authors.

SHOULD I USE A PEN NAME?

You don't have to have this figured out yet. On the other hand, if you haven't established some kind of social media presence by now, I do recommend it, and to do that, you need to know what your name is.

By the way, Bryn Donovan is my pen name. Donovan is my real last name, and Bryn comes from a favorite song of mine by the band Vampire Weekend. I'm going to go over the benefits of using a pen name and some considerations in choosing one.

Benefit #1: Get a Name You Like Better
Not everybody loves their real name. If you don't, then writing is a great opportunity to pick a new one. And if you want, you can even change the way you think about yourself...or flat-out reinvent yourself...based on that name.

Benefit #2: Own the Google Search
If you have a fairly common name and you publish under your real name, then anyone who Googles you is going to get a bunch of results about other

people. Before you become very famous, which I know you will, there will be a few years where your first fans have a hard time finding you online.

Bryn Donovan is not a common name, so if you Google it, most of the results will be about me. On the other hand, I've published one novel under my "real" name, Stacey Donovan, which I share with a very popular ex-porn star from the '80s/early '90s, as well as another writer and editor. (I want to have brunch with the other two Stacey Donovans sometime. I think that would be amazing.) Occasionally, Google itself gets confused and pairs my LinkedIn photo with the ex-porn star's biography. That always makes me laugh. My husband is less amused.

The point is, though, I don't even come close to owning the Google search there. If you have an original name, you can own the Google search, and you'll also be able to register a website domain for that name, which will be nice.

Benefit #3: Separation From Personal Life

You may want to create distance between what you do as an author and what you do in your day job or how you're known in the community. I do want to add a word of warning here, however: I don't think you should ever assume or attempt to maintain a completely secret author identity. Even if you have a pen name, it's very difficult to market books without ever showing your face, and most publishers will expect to be able to use your author photo and bio, to have you take interviews, and so on. Plus, if you're trying to hide your identity and you're writing and publishing things that would be embarrassing if everyone knew, that makes you vulnerable. Someone can dox you—in other words, publicly reveal your true identity—and mess up your life.

You only want to publish things that you stand behind and feel proud of, even if you're using a pen name.

CONSIDERATIONS WHEN CHOOSING A PEN NAME

Is it plausible?

I recommend choosing a name that sounds like it could be a real name. I think that's more professional. As an editor, when I get a manuscript with an over-the-top pen name, it doesn't make the best first impression. The same is true when I'm just shopping for books on Amazon. But hey, it's your decision.

Is it easy to pronounce?
If it's easier to pronounce, it's easier for readers to recommend to one another. Word of mouth is very important in publishing, so that might be something to consider. However, I don't think it should be the only factor. If your real name reflects your cultural heritage and you love it, though, you might want to keep it. After all, people have learned how to say Tchaikovsky and Nietzsche. They can learn how to say your name, too.

Is it short?
If you have a short pen name, it's easier for readers to remember and easier to make it big on a book cover. But again, this is all up to you. If your real name is long and you love it, keep it!

DON'T CATFISH

If you're a guy writing romance for a female audience and you want to use a female pen name, that's fine. Conversely, if you're a woman who thinks she might be taken more seriously with a male pen name, that's okay, too. Once, I had a group of poems I wasn't able to get published in literary magazines; when I began submitting them under a male pseudonym, I got acceptances right away.

However, don't come up with a whole different identity for yourself, with a fake photo, a fake biography…a fake life. This is lying. Most readers understand that many authors write under pen names, but if they learn you've misled them to this degree, they'll get angry. Ultimately, you don't want to violate the readers' trust.

PEN NAMES AND SUBMITTING

One question that comes up a lot is whether you submit to agents and publishers under a pen name or under your real name. In my own experience in publishing, I've seen writers handle this in a few different ways. Some don't mention their real name at all in the submission. Some sign the query letter with their real name and indicate that they are writing under a pen name. The pen name will usually be on the manuscript itself.

There have been times that I haven't actually known a writer's real name until we're drawing up the publishing contract. I do need to have their legal name and other identifying information at that point, because otherwise, I can't pay them.

From a publisher's perspective, I prefer to know what the pen name is so I can see the author's other books (if they have other books) and take a look at their social media presence.

CHECKLIST FOR STEP 34

☐ I've hit my word count.

☐ (optional) I've given some thought about whether I should use a pen name.

☐ I've backed up my work so far, because if I lose it, a lot of time and effort will be wasted.

STEP 35: FINISH IT!

So far in Section II, every chapter has included a mini-lesson. This chapter is different. In this step, you have one focus and one focus only: finishing the complete draft of your novel.

If you're like a lot of us, the final push can be a big one. Stock up on healthy snacks, make that extra pot of coffee, reschedule meetings, decline invitations, give up on the housework, order takeout, tell the kids they're skipping dance lessons this week…do whatever you've got to do. Get it done!

If this is your first time finishing a rough draft, let me tell you, it's one of the best feelings ever. It's also a turning point for you as a writer. Now you know that you can do it!

Even if you've written a hundred novels before, it's still a great moment. No matter what else is going on in your life, take time to enjoy that satisfaction. Yes, you still have a lot of work to do, but that doesn't change the fact that this is a milestone. Tell your friends and family so they can congratulate you. Find a way to reward yourself. Celebrate!

CHECKLIST FOR STEP 35

- [ ] I've finished my rough draft!!
- [ ] I've savored the sweet success of my accomplishment.
- [ ] (optional) I've printed it out and marveled at it.
- [ ] I've backed it up so that there's NO possibility of losing it!

SECTION III: REVISING AND EDITING

GET IT IN SHAPE!

EDITING IS MY FAVORITE PART of writing. I'm refining and improving. With every session, I clear away more of the dust, until finally, it shines.

Some people find the revision process baffling or overwhelming. That's because they try to tackle everything at once. "First I'll fix Chapter One," they think, which sounds logical enough. But Chapter One is connected to every other chapter, and they become aware of so many problems, they hardly know how to fix them all.

Instead of going chapter by chapter, we're going to take pass after pass throughout the whole manuscript, addressing one issue at a time. We'll start with broad strokes, making the story more compelling and satisfying, and eventually, we'll get to the fine-tuning.

When you revise, you have to be tough. You can't be too in love with the first draft, and you can't be too afraid of messing with it. You have to be open to the possibility of changing many things for the better. And if you find that some of your changes make the draft worse, well, you can just load your last good saved version and get it right this time.

Hopefully, if you follow this process, you'll come to enjoy it as much as I do!

STEP 36: CLARIFY THE FIRST CHARACTER ARC

When you were in the plotting stage of your novel, we talked about your main characters' arcs—in other words, the way they develop, change, and grow over the course of the story. Now that you have a finished draft, it's time to take a look at that again.

Start with your most important character. If you've got more than one main character and they're all equally important, just choose one.

Write out a paragraph to describe the character's arc. Even if you had an idea about this during the plotting stage, things may have shifted as you wrote the story. If they did, that may be a good thing! You may have learned more along the way.

Here are two examples of what that might look like.

Jinyoung is new at the moon colony, and at first, she feels scornful of the colonists' "backward" ways. Gradually, she becomes more comfortable with their culture and makes close friends. By the end of the story, she's willing to sacrifice everything to save her fellow colonists.

Matthew's boyfriend dumped him after ten years, leaving him crushed. Through Matthew's volunteer work at the animal shelter and the eccentric new friends he makes there, he gains enough confidence to ask out his coworker, Jack. When Jack considers a move across the country, Matthew pretends at first that he doesn't care, leading to a rift. A rescued dog teaches Matthew the value of risking his heart again. Matthew tells Jack he loves him, Jack stays, and they live happily ever after.

In the first example, Jinyoung's arc is learning to overcome her prejudices and bond with the community. In the second example, Matthew gradually opens himself up again to taking risks—and to love.

Do you have your paragraph written for your first main character?

Okay, great! Now you're going to take a printout of your manuscript and three highlighter pens in different colors. (I'll say yellow, pink, and green, but obviously, use whatever you've got.)

With your yellow pen, circle a scene or two near the beginning that establishes the character's original state (e.g. Jinyoung thinking the moon colonists are unsophisticated; Matthew lacking in confidence.)

With your pink pen, circle scenes in the middle part of the story that show how your character is changing.

With your green pen, circle a scene or two near the end that shows how much your character has transformed.

Are you missing the scenes in the middle? Then your character's changes may seem to come out of nowhere at the end. You may have to add something to show the growth happening more gradually. You might be creating a whole new scene or two, or you might be adding a paragraph or two in a couple of places.

Do you feel like the character's growth is too subtle? You might want to insert sentences to make it clearer. At my day job, we do this in the editing stage all the time. What's obvious to the author isn't always as obvious to the reader.

Is the character's transformation enough for you? You might want to rethink either the beginning or the ending to show more of an arc. This is a bigger revision, but if you dive into it, you may be surprised at how fast it goes.

Do whatever you need to do to show your characters' gradual transformation. You may wind up with just a little bit of writing or quite a lot of work, but either way, it's going to be worth it and make your story stronger.

CHECKLIST FOR STEP 36

- [ ] I've written out a paragraph about a main character's arc.
- [ ] I've analyzed how that arc plays out in my rough draft.
- [ ] I've made revisions to make the arc clearer and stronger.
- [ ] I've saved my work so far, which has now become an ingrained habit.

STEP 37: CLARIFY THE SECOND CHARACTER ARC

You're going to do the exact same thing you did in the previous step, except with your second most important character.

As an editor and as a reader, I've seen countless stories fall flat because only one of the characters truly grows and changes. If your two most important characters both have strong arcs, it's very likely going to make your novel a lot more satisfying to your reader.

If you have more than two point-of-view characters, you probably want to work on showing the growth and development of all of them. It's a lot more work, but if you've gotten this far, I'm sure you're up to the challenge!

CHECKLIST FOR STEP 37

- [ ] I've written a paragraph about another character's arc.
- [ ] I've analyzed how that arc plays out in my rough draft.
- [ ] I've made revisions to make the arc clearer and stronger.
- [ ] I've backed up my work so far.

STEP 38: FINE-TUNE MAIN CHARACTERS' SPEECH AND BEHAVIOR

You've clarified your main characters' arcs. In doing so, you've made not only your characters, but also your whole story, more compelling. Nice job! As writers, we always want to create stories that people won't want to put down, and this kind of revising is key to achieving that goal.

In this step, we're going to make your main characters even more believable and original by making sure everything they say and do is truly "in character." That's the *only* thing you're going to pay attention to in this pass. I've never heard of anyone else advising an editing pass like this, but for me, it makes a huge difference. Your characters become more distinctive, real, and memorable.

We'll focus on your most important characters. This is usually a time-consuming editing process, but if you have extra time, you can also make a quick pass for your secondary characters.

Your characters are individuals, so you don't want them sounding or acting just like one another. Write down a few descriptors about how each main character talks and behaves. For example, here's how I would describe the speech and behavior of two of my main characters in the same book.

Cassie
- blurts things out, sometimes putting her foot in her mouth
- curses when angry; uses coarse language in general
- often sarcastic

- high energy; can have a hard time sitting still
- says "holy smokes"
- hugs herself when upset or scared

Jonathan
- sincere
- rarely sarcastic; makes only the occasional dry observation
- rarely curses; when he does, it's mostly in Latin
- has urge to kick, smash things when angry (*mostly* keeps it in check)
- rubs his shoulder when uncomfortable

Notice how Cassie has a smart mouth, but Jonathan doesn't? Some authors with a gift for sarcasm give all of their characters sassy one-liners. The danger with this, of course, is winding up with characters who all sound the same. All of the characters can be funny…but they have to be funny in *different ways*. For instance, one of them might excel at sarcastic putdowns, another might favor self-deprecating humor, and still another might be naïve and optimistic in a way that's unintentionally funny.

If you like to work humor into a story, don't underestimate the value of a "straight man" (or woman, or non-binary character). This is the sensible or more serious character who reacts to the more eccentric or funnier one. The "straight man" is a tradition in comedy for a reason; this character amplifies the humor.

How does your main character act when they're angry? Do they lash out, cry, or silently fume? How do they behave when they're happy? They don't need to do the exact same thing every time they're angry, or every time they're happy…but there should be a thread of consistency. Look for ways to weave that through the story.

By the way, with the gestures or body language, I'm not going to overdo it. Jonathan's not going to be rubbing his shoulder on every other page. It'll just come up two or three times over the course of the story…and he'll be the only character who does it. Readers may not even consciously notice this, but it'll still make the character more consistent for them.

Once you've thought about the way your characters talk, move, and behave, you can take a pass through your manuscript for each character, honing in on their dialogue and behavior. Look for places where they're speaking too casually or too formally for their personality, revealing too much when they tend to bottle things up, or using long sentences when they usually express themselves succinctly.

OVERFAMILIAR DIALOGUE

While you're at it, look for places where your characters don't sound like themselves exactly, but like stock characters in movies. Are they saying things like this?

"You can't…or you *won't*?" (This is one of my pet peeves.)

"You're going to want to see this."

"You say that like it's a bad thing."

(When bad guys or potentially bad guys show up): "We've got company."

"You just don't get it, do you?" (This is my other pet peeve!)

(after a big interruption) "Well! Where were we?"

I could probably share a hundred or more examples of dialogue like this, but you get the idea.

If you come across overfamiliar turns of phrase and lines of dialogue like this, think about who your character is and how they would really say it. Then replace the cliché with something that's more "them."

And honestly, you may decide that in one or two places, your character *would* express themself using a familiar turn of phrase. Although I know some writers would argue with me on this one, I feel that one or two instances like this in your manuscript might be fine.

Don't feel bad if you have too many clichés in the first draft. A cliché is the thing that popped into your head first because you're well-versed in your own culture. Plenty of good writers have clichés in their first drafts. It literally does not matter. You're fixing it now.

DO WOMEN AND MEN ALWAYS SPEAK AND ACT DIFFERENTLY?

Some people will tell you that women *have* to use more qualifiers in their speech, ("I don't know, but…" "Just a thought, but…") You might also hear people say that men *can't* express their feelings directly, or never use long and complex sentences, and so on. Some may also point to studies that show how, in a group of men and women, men tend to do more of the talking.

It's true that there are some differences in the way an average woman and an average man expresses herself or himself, at least in the United States. We can make some general differences between men's and women's behavior, too. For example, statistically, men are much more prone to acts of violent aggression. There are differences in brain chemistry between men and women, but because of the way the brain is able to change itself, even these differences are influenced to a great extent by culture and socialization. (Our studies of these differences are influenced by our cultural expectations as well.)

It's good to be aware of these things, particularly if you're writing realistic contemporary fiction. But then again…your characters may not be average! And if you're writing about characters in a fantasy world, a secret cult, or a futuristic realm, gender expectations may be different. Heck, they may be nonexistent.

You can consider the way that men and women *tend* to behave differently or express themselves differently, but you can also take them with a big grain of salt…or actually, a whole salt lick of salt. Make the decisions that seem right for your story.

A FEW MORE CONSIDERATIONS

Here are a few more things you might think about as you're fine-tuning your character, if you haven't considered them already.

What's one thing your character *loves*? Frappuccinos? Perfectly tailored suits? Bring it up twice in the book.

What's one thing your character can't *stand*? Cold weather? Getting up early? Bring it up once or twice over the course of the story.

This one is optional: does your character have a particular phobia? If he does, you might want to bring that out a bit more.

Go through every scene that features your main character. Look at everything they say and do. And make them talk, act, and even think in a way that's more true to them.

Then, do the same thing with your second-most-important character. Again, whether you want to do it with additional characters is up to you.

This is one of my very favorite parts of the editing process. Even if I'm feeling burned out on my project, paying close attention to my characters and bringing out their unique personalities makes me fall in love with them—and the story—all over again. I hope you feel the same way!

WHY THIS STEP MATTERS

Because we're all different and because every project is different, you might not be loving this part. You might be asking yourself, "Why do I have to work so hard on these characters?"

Here's why: there may be no better way to win a reader's praise and loyalty than to give them characters they understand, know, and love.

You've probably read and enjoyed books that didn't have the strongest plots. You may have had the experience of continuing to watch a TV show even after it started to go downhill. Why? Because you loved the characters.

Great characters are friends to us. The fact that they're fictional doesn't change that. But for characters to feel real, we have to make sure that in their actions, words, and even thoughts, their unique personalities shine through.

In fact, here's something you might try.

A Quick Character Development Exercise
Write down five of your favorite fictional characters. They can be from books, or from TV shows or movies.

For each of them, write down one or two reasons why you *love* that character.

Look at those reasons. Do you love any of the same aspects about characters in your own novel-in-progress? Do you want to bring out those qualities? Now's the time to do it.

CHECKLIST FOR STEP 38

☐ I've made notes on my main characters' speech and behavior.

☐ I've considered my main characters' likes and dislikes.

☐ (optional) I've thought about why I love my favorite fictional characters…and whether my characters have similar qualities I want to emphasize.

☐ I've made revisions to fine-tune my main characters' speech and behavior.

☐ I've backed up my novel, because no way am I losing work now.

STEP 39: PUMP IT UP, PART I

Here's a very exciting step in the editing process. You're going to be making sure your novel has the impact you want it to have on readers and reviewers!

Let's start out with a quick exercise. It's so simple, but it can take your draft to the next level.

THE BILLBOARD FILL-IN-THE-BLANK EXERCISE

Imagine your book is published and on sale, and your publisher has decided to advertise it on billboards in cities around the country. (This isn't how most publishers advertise books, but just go with it.)

The billboard features your beautiful book cover plus a quote from a review in *The New York Times* or *Publishers Weekly*. Congratulations on the rave reviews, by the way!

And that quote says:

"A *adjective, adjective genre* novel."

Except, obviously, you have to fill in those blanks with your genre and the two adjectives you'd love that reviewer to use when describing your novel. Here are some examples of how you might do that (and obviously, you can take some liberties with the wording, as I've done.)

"A gritty, heart-pounding thriller."
"A sexy, funny romance."
"An original, spine-tingling horror story."
"A heartbreaking but ultimately hopeful young adult novel."
"A lyrical, evocative work of literary fiction."

As you do this exercise, keep the expectations of your genre in mind.

A romance novel had better be, you know, romantic. A horror story needs to scare readers. A thriller needs to thrill.

Here are examples of other adjectives you might choose for your review quote, but you can probably think of your own.

suspenseful	insightful
intriguing	smart
exciting	fast-paced
action-packed	shocking
heartwarming	unpredictable
lighthearted	edgy
tender	surreal
sweet	realistic
mesmerizing	entertaining
heroic	quirky
imaginative	charming
epic	witty
powerful	slick
engaging	glamorous
lyrical	inspiring

BRINGING YOUR DRAFT TO LIFE

Now you're going to look at the first of your two adjectives and figure out how to make changes to your draft to make it *more that way.*

If your adjective is *funny*, you're going to look for opportunities in scenes to add humor. You might add a few more witty lines of dialogue. You might even write a whole new funny scene.

If your adjective is *action-packed,* you may decide to cut back on a long scene where everyone's sitting around talking…and add a fight.

But what if your adjective is *lyrical*? That's going to be impossible, right? Nah…you can do it. Rewrite some of those descriptions and some of that exposition to make it more poetic.

If you haven't revised many novels, the idea of making a story more *emotional, dazzling, riveting,* or whatever words you chose in the editing stage may seem strange to you. You may feel like the first draft either has it, or it doesn't.

Nothing could be further from the truth. A draft can come to life in the editing stage!

STUCK? MAKE A QUICK LIST

If you have no idea what to do to your draft to achieve the effect you want, use the method I use to break through all kinds of creative problems in my writing: the Quick List Method.

At the top of the page, write your question. In this case, your question is: "How can I make this novel more inspiring?" (Or funnier, or more exciting, or whatever your adjective is.)

Number your paper 1 through 20.

Now, as fast as you can, write down answers to the question.

Don't be afraid of a few dumb answers. If you're asking yourself, "How can I make this novel more inspiring?" and the first two answers that pop into your head are "Have an eagle soar above every single scene" or "Have my main character climb Mount Everest halfway through," that's fine! Write it down! You have to write down the silly ideas to get to the good ideas.

Don't judge what you're writing, and concentrate on speed. That's the key to this brainstorming method. Get to #20 as fast as you can.

By the time you get to 20, I *bet* you'll have one to three good ideas in there.

See that? Sometimes you have to get out of your own way.

Whatever first adjective you chose, make it more of that. But don't get too overwhelmed. You don't have to change every page or every scene! Just find some opportunities to make it more of what you want it to be.

CHECKLIST FOR STEP 39

☐ I've done the Billboard Fill-In-The-Blank exercise to identify two adjectives I want people to use when describing my novel.

☐ I've focused on the first adjective, and I've made revisions to make the novel better fit the adjective.

☐ I've backed up my novel, because I have a professional attitude toward my writing.

STEP 40: PUMP IT UP, PART II

DO IT AGAIN

In this step, you're focusing on the second adjective in your future review quote. So if you wrote "A mind-blowing, adventurous work of science fiction," and you're done making it at least a bit more mind-blowing, now you can concentrate on making it more adventurous.

GET YOUR BETA READERS LINED UP

A couple of weeks from now (or much sooner, if you're going faster), you're going to need beta readers to read through your whole novel. You need to go ahead and get people signed up for this.

It's a huge time commitment on their part, so you need to bring out your best begging, bribing, and bartering skills. Tell them how smart they are and how desperately you need their opinion. Tell them you'll take in their dog while they go on vacation. Offer to give them feedback on *their* novel. Do whatever you need to do (well, within the boundaries of the law and common decency).

CHECKLIST FOR STEP 40

- [ ] I've focused on the second adjective, and I've made revisions to make the novel better fit the adjective.
- [ ] I've lined up beta readers.
- [ ] I've backed up my novel, because I'm not asking for trouble.

STEP 41: IT'S BETA READER TIME!

It's time to give your entire novel to your beta readers and get their feedback. Hopefully, because you've gotten responses from them before, it won't be too daunting to hand it over now. Of course, it's possible you fired your first beta readers for not doing a good enough job. If you're working with new ones for this round, I hope it goes better!

As you email it to them or hand them a printout, give yourself a pat on the back for all the hard work you've done. But don't hope for nothing but accolades. You need criticism. There may be issues with the story that you can't see because you're too close to it. Feedback from others will help you make your book even better.

If you're doing a step a week, tell them you need feedback in three weeks. If you're doing it faster, you can give them a shorter deadline, but faster than one week is probably too demanding.

As always, you should give them questions to answer about the manuscript. Here are some suggestions, but you might have ones that are particular to your story.

> *What did you like about the story?*
> *Did any sections bore you?*
> *Did anything annoy or confuse you?*
> *What did you think of the characters?*
> *Did you feel satisfied by the ending?*

DO YOU NEED A SENSITIVITY READER?

In Step 14, we talked about using a sensitivity reader if you want to avoid stereotypes, unintended insults, or inaccuracy about a character whose experience is much different from your own. If you need a sensitivity reader, now is the time to use one.

Never ask someone to do sensitivity reading for free. Pay them either in money or in trade (by proofreading their manuscript or providing some other service to them in exchange for their labor).

WHILE YOU'RE WAITING, CHECK YOUR POINT OF VIEW

We talked earlier about choosing point of view characters for the novel. Now is a great time to take a look at which chapters and sections are in which point of view and see if you're happy with the overall flow.

Here's how you do it. Let's pretend you have ten chapters. (Honestly, I hope you have more than that, but I want to keep this example simple.) Create a new document with Chapter One, Chapter Two, and so on, right down the page.

Now go through and make a note of whose point of view each chapter is in. Some chapters may contain more than one point of view.

Your document might look something like this:

Chapter One: Jill
Chapter Two: Marcus
Chapter Three: Jill
Chapter Four: Jill
Chapter Five: Jill/Marcus/Jill
Chapter Six: Jill
Chapter Seven: Jill
Chapter Eight: Jill/Vanessa
Chapter Nine: Jill/Marcus/Jill/Marcus
Chapter Ten: Jill

Looking back at this, I might decide a few things. For example:

In chapter five and chapter nine, the point of view is bouncing around too much. I'm going to rewrite a few of those scenes to smooth it out. And in fact, since I don't have as much of Marcus's thoughts and feelings as I'd like, I'm going to go ahead and put both of those chapters in his point of view only.

I notice, though, that by doing this, I'm going to cut out something Jill's thinking that's actually pretty important to the story. No problem! When I'm back in Jill's point of view in the next chapter, I'll add a short paragraph about her reflecting on what happened between her and Marcus. I'll insert the vital material in there.

I'm only in Vanessa's point of view for part of chapter eight, so that's kind of odd ...and it's not even necessary. I do want the reader to know what Vanessa's thinking, but I can convey it through her facial expressions, body language, and a couple of extra lines of dialogue. I'll rewrite it to put the whole chapter in Jill's point of view.

Now I wind up with only two point-of-view characters. It's mostly in Jill's point of view, but I get Marcus's point of view near the beginning, in the middle, and near the end. This feels so much better.

Changing and smoothing out your point of view choices can take some time, but once you dive into it, it might not be as daunting as it first seems. If it makes your story more balanced, it's worth it.

CHECKLIST FOR STEP 41

- [ ] I've given my novel to beta readers with specific questions for them to answer and with a deadline for feedback.
- [ ] I've analyzed the point of view in my novel and I've rewritten passages to change the point of view as necessary.
- [ ] I've backed up my novel, because I'm not letting revisions get lost.

STEP 42: WHILE YOU'RE WAITING, CHECK YOUR CHAPTER LENGTHS, CHAPTER BREAKS, AND TIMELINE

Now that the point of view is adjusted to your liking, let's take a look at chapter length and where you're breaking the chapters.

CHECKING THE CHAPTER LENGTHS

First of all, write down the page count for each of your chapters. Let's say the first ten chapters look like this.

Chapter One – 12 pages
Chapter Two – 8 pages
Chapter Three – 4 pages
Chapter Four – 5 pages
Chapter Five – 22 pages
Chapter Six – 9 pages
Chapter Seven – 7 pages
Chapter Eight – 14 pages
Chapter Nine – 10 pages
Chapter Ten – 11 pages

The lengths of your chapters vary quite a bit. That might be okay, but when you look at chapters three and four, there's no particular reason for them to be so short. In fact, chapter three doesn't have a strong ending, and both chapters are in the same point of view. So you can smoosh chapters three and four together to create one chapter.

Chapter five goes on forever. You're going to break it into two chapters if you can.

Maybe it's all one long scene, in one person's point of view. A move to a different time and/or location is a typical place to start a new chapter. However, you don't *have* to wait for a scene change to do a chapter break.

Scanning through chapter five, you might notice that something significant happens about two-thirds of the way through. You could start a new chapter right after that event.

You may still have a lot of variance in my chapter lengths, but that's fine. You just don't want so much variance that the rhythm feels unsettling to the reader...unless, of course, you have a *very* good reason for it to feel unsettling (for example, a very short chapter because your character gets unexpectedly knocked unconscious.)

TEASING THE CHAPTER ENDINGS

In Step 10, we talked about ending chapters in a way that entices readers to keep on reading. Not every chapter needs to end like that, but at least some of them probably should. This is a good time to look at the last few sentences of each chapter.

Here's an editing secret: the last sentence of a paragraph, and the last few sentences of a chapter, can sometimes be cut. Many of us writers tend to hit a strong note...and then add a little bit of unnecessary material right after that. In revision, try to end on the strong note.

You might even consider ending one or two chapters with a question.
How would I ever get there in time?
If she never showed up for basketball practice, where did she go?
Would he hate me if he learned the truth?
You may decide to put a chapter break or two in a different place altogether in order to create that little bit of suspense that keeps your reader flipping pages. You'll keep them up way too late reading so that they go to work or school groggy and sleep-deprived the next day. And because readers are a strange breed, they'll love you for it.

FIXING YOUR TIMELINE

In fiction, it's very easy to lose track of what day it is or how much time has passed. You may somehow put an extra day in between Tuesday and Wednesday, for example, or not even be sure yourself if they've been on vacation for one week or two.

To check your timeline, you write the date or dates next to each chapter. If you don't know the exact dates—for example, you figure the story happens in October and ends on Halloween—you figure out a starting date so you can check everything else.

Your first ten chapters might look like this:

Chapter One	Saturday, Oct. 5
Chapter Two	Monday, Oct. 7
Chapter Three	Monday night, Oct. 7
Chapter Four	Monday, Oct. 21
Chapter Five	Friday, Oct. 25
Chapter Six	Saturday, Oct. 26
Chapter Seven	still Saturday, Oct. 26
Chapter Eight	Monday, Oct. 28
Chapter Nine	Monday, Oct. ??
Chapter Ten	Halloween

Hmm…it turns out that near the end, you have two Mondays in the same week. You're going to have to rewrite a bit to make the timeline correct.

MAKING THE PASSAGE OF TIME CLEAR

While you're at it, go back and make sure your readers can tell where they're at in the story. See that two-week jump between chapters three and chapter four? I might address that in dialogue, soon after the chapter begins:

> "Halloween is ten days away," Josie said. "I have plenty of time to figure out a costume."

Or I might slip the time jump in there before a paragraph of action.

On the day before Halloween, Josie went into a thrift shop hoping to find something that could pass as a costume.

If I'm writing in Josie's point of view, that last option, strictly speaking, breaks her point of view. It's a slip into an omniscient voice. But because it's at the beginning of the chapter and it's so quick, I'm not worried about it.

If you're writing historical, can you put certain events—say, a New Year's lunar eclipse—in a year when no such event happened? The majority of readers won't look this kind of thing up. A few will, and you might feel better if you make it historically accurate. It's up to you.

CHECKLIST FOR STEP 42

- [ ] I've looked at my chapter lengths and I've made changes where necessary.
- [ ] I've looked at my chapter endings and I've made changes so they finish strong.
- [ ] I've looked at the timeline of my novel and I've made any necessary changes for continuity.
- [ ] I've made sure that the passage of time is clear.
- [ ] I've backed up my novel so far.

STEP 43: READ OVER YOUR FEEDBACK

It may take some prodding and nudging, but you should get your critiques back from most of your beta readers by now.

As always, some criticism may sting. Remember, if all your beta readers did was tell you how wonderful your story was, they wouldn't be doing their jobs. If you need unconditional praise on your story, that's fine, and you can assign that job to your best friend, spouse, or mom. You're relying on your beta readers to give you ways to improve your story even more.

To reduce the sting, I again recommend reading straight through all the feedback…and then not thinking about it for three days. Give your mind a break.

When you come back to the criticism, identify the three biggest things you need to fix. You'll be focusing on those three things next.

Sometimes we balk at criticism, not because we disagree with it, but because we think it's impossible to incorporate into our manuscript. Don't be so sure! Most issues that seem big are 100% fixable, and they sometimes take less time to fix than you expected. Even if you don't see how to do it right away, the solution will come to you.

If one or more of your beta readers did a lot of proofreading, hang on to those proofreading marks. You can make fixes later.

WHAT IF I CAN'T GET MY BETA READERS TO READ IT?

Lots of us have been in this situation before! The first thing you need to remember is that this isn't a reflection on the quality of your story.

If you've asked friends to do it, it may not even be a reflection on the quality of your friendships.

Your best bet is to try again with new people. If you're not in any kind of writing organization, find one. If you are, and they're the ones who let you down, try a new one. Connect with authors online and see if you can find a critique partner.

If you really can't find a beta reader, try this instead.

The Virtual Famous Beta Reader

Here's a way to get some fresh insight on your story, and it works because you're a writer and therefore have a good imagination.

Choose an author in your genre whom you admire and want to be like. Now imagine handing your manuscript over to them for critique.

Flip through your manuscript, imagining that you are that author. Do choose someone living; Charles Dickens or Jane Austen won't give you the best advice about contemporary fiction (even if your story is set in a historical era), because you're writing for contemporary readers.

Keep in mind all the things this author accomplished, the choices they made in their own books, and their particular strengths. Then, imagine what comments they'd make on yours. Would they have questions about a main character's actions? Would they suggest more vivid description? Would they be looking for something more dramatic to happen at the end?

This exercise usually isn't as good as actual beta reader feedback. However, it's something you can do by yourself, and it's a great, quick way for you to get some distance from your own work.

CHECKLIST FOR STEP 43

- [ ] I've read through my beta reader feedback...*or*...
- [ ] I've read through my manuscript while imagining what a favorite famous author would say about it.
- [ ] I've written down the three most important things about my manuscript to fix or change.

STEP 44: REVISE BASED ON BETA READER FEEDBACK, PART I

After you've gotten critiques on your whole draft, there can be a tendency to want to change everything at once. You're going to be more effective, though, if you stay focused. Concentrate on the first thing you wrote down, whether it's a pace that drags in the middle, a pesky plot hole, a frustrating ending, or occasionally clunky dialogue.

What if you're not positive a change will be an improvement? No problem. Save a version of the draft, clearly marked, that's the "old" version. Then make the changes and see if the new version is better. I've done this several times. And every single time so far, I've liked the new version better! But saving the old version will put your worries at rest and allow you to try something new with the draft.

CHECKLIST FOR STEP 44

- [ ] I've fixed the first key issue I identified with the manuscript.
- [ ] I've backed up my work.

STEPS 45 AND 46: REVISE BASED ON BETA READER FEEDBACK, PARTS II AND III

You're probably feeling a lot better about your beta reader feedback now that you've tackled one of the issues. You may have even balked at a concern or criticism at first—only to implement it and discover that it made your story shine.

Step 45 is attacking the second issue on your manuscript, and Step 46 is attacking the third one. Doing these one at a time helps you focus and makes the process a whole lot less daunting.

If you're like most of us, you may be noticing some issues with the prose. It might be saying "she looked at him" and "he looked at her" on every page, overusing dashes or ellipses, or starting way too many sentences with "I." Make a note of things like this to address later, but concentrate on the bigger issues for now.

CHECKLIST FOR STEPS 45 AND 46

- [ ] I've fixed the next two key issues I identified with the manuscript.
- [ ] I've backed up my work because it's very valuable.

STEP 47: COPYEDITING, PART I: TRIM WHERE NEEDED

By now, your story is looking a lot better. In this step, you're going to cut out the fat.

Go through your manuscript and mark passages and scenes that *might* get deleted. If you're working with a hard copy, you can use a pen, and if you're using a Word document, you can use the highlighter tool. I find the printed-out copy easier to use for this stage, but it's up to you.

Look for descriptions that go on for way too long and scenes that don't show character development or move the story forward. Are your characters having the same argument they had twenty pages ago? That's realistic, maybe, but that doesn't mean it's good storytelling. Is your story filled with your characters' random musings on everything from hand soap to handbags? Cut out the reveries that aren't as clever or unique.

If you're writing fantasy or science fiction, look for places where you've included much more backstory and information about the created world than the reader needs. The author should always know their created world inside out: it makes the story not only consistent, but convincing and immersive. However, any author in this genre should be resigned to the fact that they'll know much more about their created places, cultures, histories, and lore than will ever show up on the page.

Writers who have done a lot of research for their story often have too much information on the page as well. This happens a lot in historical fiction in particular. You spent five hours researching European medieval harvesting methods, and by God, you're going to prove it! But this isn't an algebra test: you don't need to show your work. Readers want to be entertained.

If you are way over the typical word count range for your genre, be honest with yourself. Does your story really deserve more pages than the stories of the masters in your genre? If the answer is no, you have a lot of cutting to do.

Once you've marked all the *potential* places to cut back, look back at them all and pass your final judgement. Kill some of these sentences, paragraphs, passages, and scenes.

Don't cut out a passage if it sounds amazing, it doesn't break point of view, and it speaks to a *theme* of the story. (Gillian Flynn's "cool girl" passage in *Gone Girl* is a perfect example.)

Cutting often involves extra rewriting to make the passages left behind flow into one another. Get it all done in this step!

CHECKLIST FOR STEP 47

- [ ] I've evaluated where I can trim my manuscript.
- [ ] I've made judicious cuts that improve my story.
- [ ] I've done any extra writing and rewriting necessary to smooth out the manuscript after the cutting.
- [ ] I've backed up my work so far.

STEP 48: COPYEDITING, PART II: CLEANING UP

In this step, you're going to be doing a *whole lot* of cleaning up. This is the finicky part of the process, and I love it. It's so satisfying to see how dozens and dozens of tiny changes add up to make a better read.

If this isn't your favorite, though, give yourself a little reward after finishing your checklist for this step! We're going to address three separate issues here.

CLEAN UP YOUR DIALOGUE TAGS

Just as a reminder, a "dialogue tag" is any clause that tells you who's talking — *she said, he bellowed*, and so on. The way you handle dialogue tags makes a big difference in the way your story reads.

First of all, you're going to make sure you're formatting dialogue correctly throughout your manuscript. If you need a refresher course on that, go back to Step 10.

Beyond that, you're going to be fixing four common issues here.

There Are Too Many Synonyms for Said and Asked

Although we covered this in Step 10 as well, you may still have too many synonyms for said and asked—*he stated, she remarked, he questioned, she inquired,* and so on. Readers skim right over "said" and "asked," while the synonyms stand out and interrupt the flow.

As I've said, you can use them once in a while. They're especially useful when the tone of voice doesn't match what's being said. For instance:

"How delightful," he growled.

There Are Big Blocks of Nothing But Dialogue

In most cases, you want to avoid this. You're writing a novel, not a screenplay, and if you have nothing but lines of dialogue, your scene is going to feel rushed. In addition to facial expressions, body language, gestures, and actions, you can also include bits of description of the sights and sounds around your characters. If they're flirting at a backyard party, other guests might be splashing in the pool; if they're screaming at each other at home, the dog might run out of the room.

There Are Too Many Adverbs Modifying the Dialogue

We discussed this issue in Step 26. Look for places where adverbs modify dialogue tags, like this:

"I hate waffles," he said grouchily.

"Never mind, then," she said lightly.

Eliminate most of these adverbs by either cutting them out altogether or using body language, facial expressions, or gestures to convey the tone of the comment—or cutting the adverb altogether if the tone is already apparent.

"I hate waffles," he said.

She smiled and shrugged. "Never mind, then."

Unnecessary Dialogue Tags

Using dialogue tags where they aren't needed makes your story clunkier. If this is an issue in your story, here are two ways to address it.

The first way is to look for places where they can be cut. Remember, if you have a conversation between two people, you can go back and forth a few times without your reader getting lost.

The second way is to replace the dialogue tag with a facial expression, body language, gesture, or action, as in the example above with the smile and the shrug. Here are a couple more examples of this.

She scrunched up her face. "What is that?"

He grabbed his backpack. "I'm late."

If you need help with facial expressions, body language, and gestures, I have long lists of them in my book *Master Lists for Writers*. Many writers use it every day!

Missing Dialogue Tags

This is the opposite of the issue above. You never want the reader to have to guess at who's saying a line of dialogue, so look for places where this is confusing and fix them.

Inverted Dialogue Tags

As a reminder, an inverted dialogue tag is like this: *said John*

A standard dialogue tag is like this: *John said*

I recommend changing all inverted dialogue tags, for reasons outlined in Step 10.

ELIMINATE MOST INSTANCES OF PASSIVE VOICE

We covered passive voice in Step 32, and I recommend rereading that chapter if necessary. You can check for passive voice in your manuscript by searching for the word "was" (or "is," if you're writing in present tense) and then analyzing the sentences to see if it's in passive voice. Remember, in many cases, the sentences *won't* be passive voice. However, in some cases, you'll find there's a more vivid verb to use in place of "is/was," anyway.

REPLACE MANY WEAK VERBS

In Step 32, I shared examples of sentences where "was" is a weak verb and gave advice on how to make them stronger. Here are other weak verbs that may indicate an opportunity to write a better sentence. (I'm using the past tense here, but obviously, change them to present tense if your story is in present tense.)

seemed

"Martha seemed to be in a good mood as she dusted the stairwell."
Let's show instead of tell:
"Martha hummed to herself, smiling, as she dusted the stairwell."

felt

"Dev felt relieved."

Let's make that more vivid.

"Dev exhaled in relief."

looked

"The room looked warm and inviting."

We can improve this one quite a bit with more specific description.

"An overstuffed armchair sat next to the hearth, where a small fire crackled."

Look for other "filtering" verbs that put distance between the reader and the story. As a reminder, common filtering verbs include *thought, wondered, knew, realized, remembered, imagined, decided, believed, noticed, saw,* and *heard.* You can re-read Step 16 for a longer explanation of these.

Remember, you don't have to get rid of *all* weak verbs or filtering verbs! You're just looking at those sentences and making your own decision about whether there's a way to improve.

CHECKLIST FOR STEP 48

- [ ] I've cleaned up my dialogue tags.
- [ ] I've eliminated instances of passive voice except where I think I really need it.
- [ ] In many instances, I've replaced a weak and filtering verb to strengthen the sentences.
- [ ] Because I'd be despondent over losing these improvements, I've backed up my work so far.

STEP 49: COPYEDITING, PART III: QUIT REPEATING YOURSELF

All writers have certain words they overuse in the course of writing a first draft. It's nothing to be embarrassed about! It is, however, something you want to fix.

Crutch words and phrases vary from author to author. However, some common ones include: *just, so, almost, well, a little, a lot, definitely, maybe, obviously, started to, began to, suddenly, that* (often used where it's not needed), and *very*. In this book you're reading right now, I cut out many instances of *really*.

If you've never watched *Dead Poets Society*—a movie I love—I highly recommend checking it out. In one of my favorite scenes, the character played by Robin Williams delivers a great speech on avoiding the word "very."

Also look at your character's facial expressions, gestures, and reactions. Are they smiling and nodding all the time? Are they laughing at too many things, like a laugh track on a sitcom gone way out of control? Is every single character able to raise one eyebrow—and is someone doing that on every other page? Do you have a character who won't stop sighing? Eliminating these kinds of repetition will make the story you've worked so hard on more enjoyable to read.

CHECKLIST FOR STEP 49

- [ ] I've cut way back on my "crutch" words.
- [ ] I've cut way back on repeated facial expressions, gestures, and reactions.
- [ ] I've backed up my work so far so that I don't lose these great edits.

STEP 50: COPYEDITING, PART IV: READ ALOUD AND FIX AS YOU GO

In this step, you're going to read your entire novel aloud and make your final fixes as you go. Why do this? Because reading your work aloud can make you more aware of mistakes.

Of course, the best way to become aware of these mistakes would be to read your entire novel out loud to a large audience. But I'm going to assume that's not a possibility for most of us right now. So you might want to try one of these hacks instead.

*Imagine you're reading it aloud in front of a large audience.

*Imagine you're being recorded for the audiobook version.

*Actually record yourself reading it aloud. Even though you're not planning on sharing the recording with anyone else, this can make you more mindful.

*Read it aloud to your pet.

If reading your work aloud—even in an empty room—makes you nervous, you're not the only one. When I started writing, I could barely manage it. It becomes much easier with practice, and it'll help you both with edits now and with your career as an author later, when people invite you to give readings of your work.

This is going to take some time. Most likely, it'll be somewhere in between eight and twenty hours, depending on the length of your novel, your reading speed, and how quickly you make changes. I recommend doing only one or two hours at a time so that your editing brain stays alert.

CHECKLIST FOR STEP 50

☐ I've read my whole novel out loud, making final fixes in the process.

☐ I've backed up my work so far.

STEP 51: SEND IT TO PROOFREADING

Way back in Step 17, I suggested that you start saving for a proofreader if you intended to hire a professional one. There are ways to get free proofreading of your work, such as trading manuscripts with another author. Before you entrust the novel you've labored over to a proofreader, make sure you're confident in their skills for this all-important final step.

If you're hiring a professional proofreader, you can ask for references and a resume and follow up with them to make sure the person has a track record of quality work.

Before handing your novel off to the proofreader, fix any proofreading marks from your beta readers. You'll still need this final proofreading step since your book has changed since your beta readers first saw it.

You and your proofreader should agree on the payment, if applicable, and also agree on the deadline. A one-week turnaround is fast; any faster than that is a rush job. Most proofreaders use Track Changes on a Word document. This means that when you get the manuscript back, you'll be able to clearly see what changes they made and be able to accept them one by one.

Have the proofreader confirm that they've received your novel and that they're able to open the document. If you don't receive your proofreading marks by the due date, reach out the day after and ask when you can expect to get them.

CHECKLIST FOR STEP 51

☐ I've hired a proofreader.

☐ I've reached an agreement with the proofreader on the payment, the way the proofreading will be done (such as with Track Changes), and the due date.

☐ I've gotten the proofreader to confirm that they received my novel and were able to open the document.

STEP 52: GET TO YOUR FINAL DRAFT!

THIS IS IT...THE MOMENT YOU'VE been waiting for! You're getting to your final draft!

When you get your novel back from the proofreader, go through it change by change and make all of the fixes you agree with. If you're not sure what's correct, consult the *Chicago Manual of Style*.

If you're going to submit the book to agents or editors, know that once you get an interested agent or editor, they may request additional changes to the book. That's normal! The important thing here is that you've created a draft that's polished enough to showcase your talents as a writer and storyteller.

BACK UP YOUR NOVEL AND PRINT IT OUT

All throughout this book, I've been reminding you to back up your novel. Now that it's complete, saving it is paramount. Save one copy in your usual way and back it up in your usual way. I recommend printing out a copy and dating it as well.

WHAT IF I'M SELF-PUBLISHING?

If you're submitting to agents and editors, you've probably done all the proofreading you need to do. It's in pretty good shape, and publishers will proofread your work again (two or three more times, in most cases).

If you're self-publishing, you'll need at least a second proofreading pass after the book is formatted as an eBook, paperback, or both. This is because you're acting as the publisher as well as the author, and some mistakes don't jump out at the reader until the story is in book form.

DO I NEED TO COPYRIGHT MY NOVEL?

If you're in the U.S. and you are self-publishing your novel, I recommend filing for U.S. copyright. Having the copyright registration number can be helpful in pursuing a plagiarism or piracy claim.

If you're going the traditional publishing route, you don't need to file for copyright yet. The publisher usually does this.

CELEBRATE!

I said at the beginning of this book that you should alter and adjust this program to fit your needs. However, I need to tell you this:

Celebrating is a very important step. You *must not* skip it.

You've worked so hard. Writing is a tough endeavor, with only a few opportunities to celebrate. This is one of them. Take advantage of it. Bask in it.

Share a photo of your printed-out copy of your novel and let everyone on social media know about your victory.

Set up a party: in-person or virtual, depending on the situation.

Buy yourself something as a special reward.

Pop open a bottle of good champagne, if that's your style.

If it's possible, take tomorrow off and do absolutely nothing.

This might be your first, your tenth, or your thirtieth completed novel. No matter which it is, you've achieved something that many, many people want to do…and don't actually accomplish.

You have my personal congratulations for getting it done. If you're on Twitter, please tag me and let me know about your achievement using the *Blank Page to Final Draft* program…I'd love to cheer for you! Your friends and family should be proud of you, and you should be proud of yourself.

And best of all? You have more stories and more successes in the future. You're only getting started.

ABOUT THE AUTHOR

Bryn Donovan is the pen name of Stacey Donovan, the author of several romance novels, children's books, gift books, and nonfiction books, including *Master Lists for Writers* and *5,000 Writing Prompts*. She blogs about writing and positivity at bryndonovan.com. She has an MFA in Creative Writing from the University of Arizona and she works in publishing. An eternal optimist, she believes in being your true self, expressing yourself creatively, and not letting anyone set limits for you.

Made in the USA
Monee, IL
24 October 2022